MW00848861

THIRTEEN YEARS AT THE RUSSIAN COURT

Copyright © 2018 Read Books Ltd.
This book is copyright and may not be
reproduced or copied in any way without
the express permission of the publisher in writing

British Library Cataloguing-in-Publication Data
A catalogue record for this book is available from
the British Library

IN CAPTIVITY AT TSARSKOÏE-SELO
March to August, 1917

THE CZAR CLEARING A PATH THROUGH THE SNOW IN THE PARK OF
TSARSKOÏE-SELO AT THE END OF MARCH, 1917.

THIRTEEN YEARS AT THE RUSSIAN COURT

(A Personal Record of the Last Years and
Death of the Czar Nicholas II. and his Family)

BY
PIERRE GILLIARD
(Formerly Tutor to the Czarevitch)

TRANSLATED BY
F. APPLEBY HOLT, O.B.E.

WITH 59 ILLUSTRATIONS

THIRD EDITION

INTRODUCTION

IN September, 1920, after staying three years in Siberia, I was able to return to Europe. My mind was still full of the poignant drama with which I had been closely associated, but I was also still deeply impressed by the wonderful serenity and flaming faith of those who had been its victims.

Cut off from communication with the rest of the world for many months, I was unfamiliar with recent publications on the subject of the Czar Nicholas II. and his family. I was not slow to discover that though some of these works revealed a painful anxiety for accuracy and their authors endeavoured to rely on serious records (although the information they gave was often erroneous or incomplete so far as the Imperial family was concerned), the majority of them were simply a tissue of absurdities and falsehoods—in other words, vulgar outpourings exploiting the most unworthy calumnies.[1]

I was simply appalled to read some of them. But my indignation was far greater when I realised to my amazement that they had been accepted by the general public.

To rehabilitate the moral character of the Russian sovereigns was a duty—a duty called for by honesty and justice. I decided at once to attempt the task.

---

[1] To give some idea of what I mean, it is only necessary to record that in one of these books (which is based on the evidence of an *eyewitness* of the drama of Ekaterinburg, the authenticity of which is guaranteed) there is a description of my death ! All the rest is on a par.

Everyone desiring information about the end of the reign of Nicholas II. should read the remarkable articles recently published in the *Revue des Deux Mondes* by M. Paleologue, the French Ambassador at Petrograd.

Introduction

What I am endeavouring to describe is the drama of a lifetime, a drama I (at first) suspected under the brilliant exterior of a magnificent Court, and then realised personally during our captivity when circumstances brought me into intimate contact with the sovereigns. The Ekaterinburg drama was, in fact, nothing but the fulfilment of a remorseless destiny, the climax of one of the most moving tragedies humanity has known. In the following pages I shall try to show its nature and to trace its melancholy stages.

There were few who suspected this secret sorrow, yet it was of vital importance from a historical point of view. The illness of the Czarevitch cast its shadow over the whole of the concluding period of the Czar Nicholas II.'s reign and alone can explain it. Without appearing to be, it was one of the main causes of his fall, for it made possible the phenomenon of Rasputin and resulted in the fatal isolation of the sovereigns who lived in a world apart, wholly absorbed in a tragic anxiety which had to be concealed from all eyes.

In this book I have endeavoured to bring Nicholas II. and his family back to life. My aim is to be absolutely impartial and to preserve complete independence of mind in describing the events of which I have been an eyewitness. It may be that in my search for truth I have presented their political enemies with new weapons against them, but I greatly hope that this book will reveal them as they really were, for it was not the glamour of their Imperial dignity which drew me to them, but their nobility of mind and the wonderful moral grandeur they displayed through all their sufferings.

PIERRE GILLIARD.

CONTENTS

LIST OF ILLUSTRATIONS

List of Illustrations

List of Illustrations

CHAPTER I

MY FIRST LESSONS AT THE COURT

(AUTUMN, 1905)

Thirteen Years at the Russian Court

CHAPTER I

MY FIRST LESSONS AT THE COURT
(AUTUMN, 1905)

IN the autumn of 1904 I accepted a proposal which had been made to me to go to Duke Sergius of Leuchtenberg as French professor.

My pupil's father, Duke George of Leuchtenberg, was the grandson of Eugène de Beauharnais ; through his mother, the Grand-Duchess Marie Nicolaïevna, daughter of Nicholas I., he was a cousin of the Czar Nicholas II.

At the time the family were at the small estate they possessed on the shores of the Black Sea. They spent the whole winter there. It was there that we were surprised by the tragic events of the spring of 1905 and passed through many a poignant hour owing to the revolt of the Black Sea Fleet, the bombardment of the coast, the series of pogroms, and the violent acts of repression which followed. From the very start Russia showed herself to me under a terrible and menacing aspect, a presage of the horrors and sufferings she had in store for me.

At the beginning of June the family took up their residence in the attractive Villa Sergievskaïa Datcha, which the Duke possessed at Peterhof. The contrast was most striking as we

left the barren coast of the southern Crimea, with its little
Tatar villages snuggling in the mountains and its dusty
cypresses, for the splendid forests and delicious fresh breezes
of the shores of the Gulf of Finland.

Peterhof had been the favourite residence of its founder,
Peter the Great. It was there that he rested from the exhausting work of building St. Petersburg, the city which at his
command rose from the marshes at the mouth of the Neva as if
by enchantment—a city destined to rival the great European
capitals.

Everything about Peterhof recalls its creator. First of all
there is Marly in which he resided for some time—a " maison-
nette " out in the water on an isthmus of land separating two
great lakes. Then comes the Hermitage, by the shores of the
gulf where he liked to treat his helpers to banquets where the
wine flowed freely. There is Monplaisir, a building in the
Dutch style with a terrace sheer above the sea. It was his
favourite residence. How curious that this "landsman"
loved the sea so much ! Last comes the Great Palace, which,
with its lakes and the superb views in its park, he meant to
rival the splendours of Versailles.

All these buildings, with the exception of the Great Palace,
produce the impression of those abandoned, empty edifices
which memories of the past alone can bring to life.

The Czar Nicholas II. had inherited his ancestors'
preference for this delicious spot, and every summer he
brought his family to the little Alexandria Cottage in the
centre of a wooded park which sheltered it from prying
eyes.

The Duke of Leuchtenberg's family spent the entire summer
of 1905 at Peterhof. Intercourse between Alexandria and

Sergievskaïa Datcha was lively, for the Czarina and the Duchess of Leuchtenberg were on terms of the closest friendship. I was thus able to get occasional glimpses of the members of the royal family.

When my time ran out it was suggested that I should stay on as tutor to my pupil and at the same time teach French to the Grand-Duchesses Olga Nicolaïevna and Tatiana Nicolaïevna, the two elder daughters of the Czar Nicholas II. I agreed, and after a short visit to Switzerland I returned to Peterhof in the early days of September. A few weeks later I took up my new duties at the Imperial Court.

On the day appointed for my first lesson a royal carriage came to take me to Alexandria Cottage, where the Czar and his family were residing. Yet in spite of the liveried coachman, the Imperial arms on the panels, and the orders with regard to my arrival which had no doubt been given, I learned to my cost that it was no easy task to enter the residence of Their Majesties. I was stopped at the park gates, and there were several minutes of discussion before I was allowed to go in. On turning a corner I soon observed two small brick buildings connected by a covered bridge. If the carriage had not stopped I should not have known I had arrived at my destination.

I was taken up to a small room, soberly furnished in the English style, on the second storey. The door opened and the Czarina came in, holding her daughters Olga and Tatiana by the hand. After a few pleasant remarks she sat down at the table and invited me to take a place opposite her. The children sat at each end.

The Czarina was still a beautiful woman at that time. She was tall and slender and carried herself superbly. But all this ceased to count the moment one looked into her eyes—those speaking, grey-blue eyes which mirrored the emotions of a sensitive soul.

Olga, the eldest of the Grand-Duchesses, was a girl of ten, very fair, and with sparkling, mischievous eyes and a slightly *retroussé* nose. She examined me with a look which seemed from the first moment to be searching for the weak point in my armour, but there was something so pure and frank about the child that one liked her staight off.

The second girl, Tatiana, was eight and a half. She had auburn hair and was prettier than her sister, but gave òne the impression of being less transparent, frank, and spontaneous.

The lesson began. I was amazed, even embarrassed, by the very simplicity of a scene I had anticipated would be quite different. The Czarina followed everything I said very closely. I distinctly felt that I was not so much giving a lesson as undergoing an examination. The contrast between anticipation and reality quite disconcerted me. To crown my discomfort, I had had an idea that my pupils were much more advanced than they actually were. I had selected certain exercises, but they proved far too difficult. The lesson I had prepared was useless, and I had to improvise and resort to expedients. At length, to my great relief, the clock struck the hour and put an end to my ordeal.

In the weeks following the Czarina was always present at the children's lessons, in which she took visible interest. Quite frequently, when her daughters had left us, she would discuss with me the best means and methods of teaching modern languages, and I was always struck by the shrewd good sense of her views.

Of those early days I have preserved the memory of a lesson I gave a day or two previous to the issue of the Manifesto of

THE CZAREVITCH IN THE PARK OF TSARSKOÏE-SELO.
WINTER OF 1908.

THE FOUR GRAND-DUCHESSES. (CRIMEA, 1909.)
(From left to right : Anastasie, Tatiana, Marie, Olga).

[Facing page 23.

October, 1905, which summoned the Duma.   The Czarina was sitting in a low chair near the window.   She struck me instantly as absent-minded and preoccupied.   In spite of all she could do, her face betrayed her inward agitation.   She made obvious efforts to concentrate her thoughts upon us, but soon relapsed into a melancholy reverie in which she was utterly lost.   Her work slipped from her fingers to her lap. She had clasped her hands, and her gaze, following her thoughts, seemed lost and indifferent to the things about her.

I had made a practice, when the lesson was over, of shutting my book and waiting until the Czarina rose as a signal for me to retire.   This time, notwithstanding the silence which followed the end of the lesson, she was so lost in thought that she did not move.   The minutes passed and the children fidgeted.   I opened my book again and went on reading.   Not for a quarter of an hour, when one of the Grand-Duchesses went up to her mother, did she realise the time.

After a few months the Czarina appointed one of her ladies-in-waiting, Princess Obolensky, to take her place during my lessons.   She thus marked the end of the kind of trial to which I had been subjected.   I must admit the change was a relief. I was far more at my ease in Princess Obolensky's presence, and besides, she gave me devoted help.   Yet of those first months I have preserved a vivid recollection of the great interest which the Czarina, a mother with a high sense of duty, took in the education and training of her children.   Instead of the cold and haughty Empress of which I had heard so much, I had been amazed to find myself in the presence of a woman wholly devoted to her maternal obligations.

It was then, too, that I learned to realise by certain signs that the reserve which so many people had taken as an affront and had made her so many enemies was rather the effect of a natural timidity, as it were—a mask covering her sensitiveness.

I will give one detail which illustrates the Czarina's anxious interest in the upbringing of her children and the importance she attached to their showing respect for their teachers by observing that sense of decorum which is the first element of politeness. While she was present at my lessons, when I entered the room I always found the books and notebooks piled neatly in my pupils' places at the table, and I was never kept waiting a moment. It was the same afterwards. In due course my first pupils, Olga and Tatiana, were joined by Marie, in 1907, and Anastasie, in 1909, as soon as these two younger daughters had reached their ninth year.[1]

The Czarina's health, already tried by her anxiety about the menace hanging over the Czarevitch's head, by degrees prevented her from following her daughters' education. At the time I did not realise what was the cause of her apparent indifference, and was inclined to censure her for it, but it was not long before events showed me my mistake.

---

[1] It was in 1909 that my duties as tutor to Duke Sergius of Leuchtenberg came to an end. I had thus more time for my duties at the Court.

CHAPTER II

ALEXIS NICOLAïEVITCH—VISITS TO THE CRIMEA
(AUTUMN, 1911, AND SPRING, 1912)

SPALA (AUTUMN, 1912)

CHAPTER II

ALEXIS NICOLAÏEVITCH—VISITS TO THE CRIMEA
(AUTUMN, 1911, AND SPRING, 1912)

SPALA (AUTUMN, 1912)

THE Imperial family used regularly to spend the winter at Tsarskoïe-Selo, a pretty little country town some thirteen miles south of Petrograd. It stands on a hill at the top of which is the Great Palace, a favourite residence of Catherine II. Not far away is a much more modest building, the Alexander Palace, half hidden in trees of a park studded with little artificial lakes. The Czar Nicholas II. had made it one of his regular residences ever since the tragic events of January, 1905.

The Czar and Czarina occupied the ground floor of one wing and their children the floor above. The central block comprised state apartments and the other wing was occupied by certain members of the suite.

It was there that I saw the Czarevitch, Alexis Nicolaïevitch, then a baby of eighteen months old, for the first time, and under the following circumstances. As usual, I had gone that day to the Alexander Palace, where my duties called me several times a week. I was just finishing my lesson with Olga Nicolaïevna when the Czarina entered the room, carrying the son and heir. She came towards us, and evidently wished to show the one

25

member of the family I did not yet know.   I could see she was transfused by the delirious joy of a mother who at last has seen her dearest wish fulfilled.   She was proud and happy in the beauty of her child.   The Czarevitch was certainly one of the handsomest babies one could imagine, with his lovely fair curls and his great blue-grey eyes under their fringe of long curling lashes.   He had the fresh pink colour of a healthy child, and when he smiled there were two little dimples in his chubby cheeks.   When I went near him a solemn, frightened look came into his eyes, and it took a good deal to induce him to hold out a tiny hand.

At that first meeting I saw the Czarina press the little boy to her with the convulsive movement of a mother who always seems in fear of her child's life.   Yet with her the caress and the look which accompanied it revealed a secret apprehension so marked and poignant that I was struck at once.   I had not very long to wait to know its meaning.

During the years following I had increasing opportunities of seeing Alexis Nicolaïevitch, who made a practice of escaping from his sailor nurse and running into his sisters' schoolroom, from which he was soon fetched.   And yet at times his visits would suddenly cease, and for quite a considerable period he was seen no more.   Every time he disappeared everyone in the palace was smitten with the greatest depression.   My pupils betrayed it in a mood of melancholy they tried in vain to conceal.   When I asked them the cause, they answered evasively that Alexis Nicolaïevitch was not well.   I knew from other sources that he was a prey to a disease which was only mentioned inferentially and the nature of which no one ever told me.

As I have already said, when I was released from my duties

THE CZAREVITCH AT THE AGE OF FIFTEEN MONTHS. (1905.)

[Facing page 26.

THE CZARINA, A FEW MONTHS BEFORE HER MARRIAGE.
SUMMER OF 1894.

as tutor to Duke Sergius-of Leuchtenberg in 1909 I could give more time to the Grand-Duchesses. I lived in St. Petersburg and visited Tsarskoïe-Selo five times a week. Although the number of lessons I gave had considerably increased, my pupils made but slow progress, largely because the Imperial family spent months at a time in the Crimea. I regretted more and more that they had not been given a French governess, and each time they returned I always found they had forgotten a good deal. Mademoiselle Tioutcheva, their Russian governess, could not do everything, for all her intense devotion and perfect knowledge of languages. It was with a view to overcoming this difficulty that the Czarina asked me to accompany the family when they left Tsarskoïe-Selo for a considerable time.

My first visit under the new dispensation was to the Crimea in the autumn of 1911. I lived in the little town of Yalta, with my colleague, M. Petrof, professor of Russian, who had also been asked to continue his course of teaching. We went to Livadia every day to give our lessons.

The kind of life we led was extremely agreeable, for out of working hours we were absolutely free, and could enjoy the beautiful climate of the " Russian Riviera " without having to observe the formalities of Court life.

In the spring of the following year the family again spent several months in the Crimea. M. Petrof and I were lodged in a little house in the park of Livadia. We took our meals with some of the officers and officials of the Court, only the suite and a few casual visitors being admitted to the Imperial luncheon-table. In the evening the family dined quite alone.

A few days after our arrival, however, as the Czarina wished (as I subsequently ascertained) to give a delicate proof of her esteem for those to whom she was entrusting the education of her children, she instructed the Court Chamberlain to invite us to the Imperial table.

I was highly gratified by the feelings which had prompted this kindness, but these meals meant a somewhat onerous obligation, at any rate at the start, although Court etiquette was not very exacting in ordinary times.

My pupils, too, seemed to get tired of these long luncheons, and we were all glad enough to get back to the schoolroom to our afternoon lessons and simple, friendly relations. I seldom saw Alexis Nicolaïevitch. He almost always took his meals with the Czarina, who usually stayed in her own apartments.

On June 10th we returned to Tsarskoïe-Selo, and shortly afterwards the Imperial family went to Peterhof, from which they proceeded to their annual cruise in the fjords of Finland on the *Standard*.

At the beginning of September, 1912, the family left for the Forest of Bielovesa,[1] where they spent a fortnight, and then proceeded to Spala [2] for a longer visit. M. Petrof and I joined them there at the end of September. Shortly after my arrival the Czarina told me she wanted me to take Alexis Nicolaïevitch also. I gave him the first lesson on October 2nd in the presence of his mother. The child was then eight and a half. He did not know a word of French, and at first I had a good deal of difficulty. My lessons were soon interrupted, as the boy, who had looked to me ill from the outset, soon had to take to his bed. Both my colleague and myself had been struck by his

---

[1] An Imperial sporting estate in the Government of Grodno. This forest and the Caucasus are the only places where the aurochs, or European bison, is found. They still rove these immense forests, which occupy an area of more than three thousand acres.

[2] An ancient hunting-seat of the kings of Poland.

lack of colour and the fact that he was carried as if he could not walk.[1] The disease from which he was suffering had evidently taken a turn for the worse.

A few days later it was whispered that his condition was giving rise to extreme anxiety, and that Professors Rauchfuss and Fiodrof had been summoned from St. Petersburg. Yet life continued as before ; one shooting-party succeeded another, and the guests were more numerous than ever.

One evening after dinner the Grand-Duchesses Marie and Anastasie Nicolaïevna gave two short scenes from the *Bourgeois Gentilhomme* in the dining-room before Their Majesties, the suite, and several guests. I was the prompter, concealed behind a screen which did duty for the wings. By craning my neck a little I could see the Czarina in the front row of the audience smiling and talking gaily to her neighbours.

When the play was over I went out by the service door and found myself in the corridor opposite Alexis Nicolaïevitch's room, from which a moaning sound came distinctly to my ears. I suddenly noticed the Czarina running up, holding her long and awkward train in her two hands. I shrank back against the wall, and she passed me without observing my presence. There was a distracted and terror-stricken look in her face. I returned to the dining-room. The scene was of the most animated description. Footmen in livery were handing round refreshments on salvers. Everyone was laughing and exchanging jokes. The evening was at its height.

A few minutes later the Czarina came back. She had resumed the mask and forced herself to smile pleasantly at the guests who crowded round her. But I had noticed that the

---

[1] He was generally carried by Derevenko, formerly a sailor on the Imperial yacht *Standard,* to whom this duty had been assigned several years before.

Czar, even while engaged in conversation, had taken up a position from which he could watch the door, and I caught the despairing glance which the Czarina threw him as she came in. An hour later I returned to my room, still thoroughly upset at the scene which had suddenly brought home to me the tragedy of this double life.

Yet, although the invalid's condition was still worse, life had apparently undergone no change. All that happened was that we saw less and less of the Czarina. The Czar controlled his anxiety and continued his shooting-parties, while the usual crowd of guests appeared at dinner every evening.

On October 17th Professor Fiodrof arrived from St. Petersburg at last. I caught sight of him for a moment in the evening. He looked very worried. The next day was Alexis Nicolaïevitch's birthday. Apart from a religious service, there was nothing to mark the occasion. Everyone followed Their Majesties' example and endeavoured to conceal his or her apprehensions.

On October 19th the fever was worse, reaching 102·5° in the morning and 103·3° in the evening. During dinner the Czarina had Professor Fiodrof fetched. On Sunday, October 20th, the patient's condition was still worse. There were, however, a few guests at luncheon. The next day, as the Czarevitch's temperature went up to 105° and the heart was very feeble, Count Fredericks asked the Czar's permission to publish bulletins. The first was sent to St. Petersburg the same evening.

Thus the intervention of the highest official at Court had been necessary before the decision to admit the gravity of the Czarevitch's condition was taken.

Why did the Czar and Czarina subject themselves to this

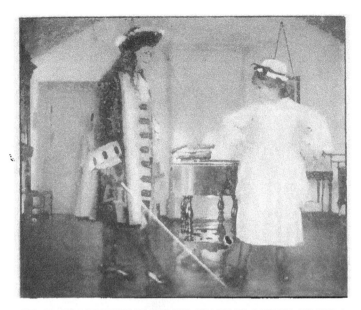

THE GRAND-DUCHESSES MARIE AND ANASTASIE DRESSED UP FOR A
SCENE FROM THE "BOURGEOIS GENTILHOMME." SPALA, AUTUMN
OF 1912.

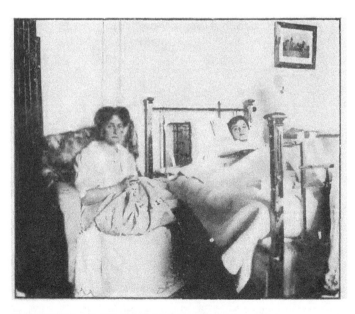

THE CZARINA AT THE CZAREVITCH'S BEDSIDE DURING HIS SEVERE
ATTACK OF HÆMOPHILIA AT SPALA IN THE AUTUMN OF 1912.

[*Facing page* 30.

dreadful ordeal ? Why, when their one desire in life was to be with their suffering son, did they force themselves to appear among their guests with a smile on their lips ? The reason was that they did not wish the world to know the nature of the Heir's illness, and, as I knew'myself, regarded it in the light of a state secret.

On the morning of October 22nd the child's temperature was 103·5°. About midday, however, the pains gradually subsided, and the doctors could proceed to a more thorough examination of the invalid, who had hitherto refused to allow it on account of his terrible sufferings.

At three o'clock in the afternoon there was a religious service in the forest. It was attended by a large number of peasants from the surrounding districts.

Beginning on the previous day, prayers for the recovery of the Heir were said twice a day. As there was no church at Spala, a tent with a small portable altar had been erected in the park as soon as we arrived. The priest officiated there morning and night.

After a few days, during which we were all a prey to the most terrible apprehensions, the crisis was reached and passed, and the period of convalescence began. It was a long and slow business, however, and we could feel that, notwithstanding the change for the better, there was still cause for anxiety. As the patient's condition required constant and most careful watching, Professor Fiodrof had sent for Dr. Vladimir Derevenko,[1] one of his young assistants, from St. Petersburg. This gentleman henceforth remained in constant attendance on the Czarevitch.

---

[1] He had the same surname as Derevenko, the sailor whom I have mentioned above. A constant cause of confusion.

The newspapers about this time had a good deal to say of the young Heir's illness—and the most fantastic stories were going round. I only had the truth some time later, and then from Dr. Derevenko himself. The crisis had been brought on by a fall of Alexis Nicolaïevitch at Bielovesa. In trying to get out of a boat he had hit his left thigh on the side, and the blow had caused rather profuse internal hæmorrhage. He was just getting better when some imprudence at Spala suddenly aggravated his condition. A sanguineous tumour formed in the groin and nearly produced a serious infection.

On November 16th it was possible to think of removing the child, without too great danger of relapse but with extreme care, from Spala to Tsarskoïe-Selo, where the Imperial family passed the entire winter.

Alexis Nicolaïevitch's condition required assiduous and special medical attention. His illness at Spala had left behind it a temporary atrophy of the nerves of the left leg, which remained drawn up and could not be straightened out by the boy himself. Massage and orthopedic appliances were necessary, but in time these measures brought the limb back to its normal position.

It is hardly necessary to say that under these circumstances I could not even think of resuming my work with the Czarevitch. This state of things lasted until the summer holidays of 1913.

I was in the habit of visiting Switzerland every summer. That year the Czarina informed me a few days before I left that on my return she proposed to appoint me tutor to Alexis Nicolaïevitch. The news filled me with a mingled sense of pleasure and apprehension. I was delighted at the confidence shown in me, but nervous of the responsibility it involved.

Yet I felt I had no right to try and escape the heavy task assigned to me, as circumstances might enable me to exercise some influence, however slight, on the intellectual development of the boy who would one day be the ruler of one of the mightiest states of Europe.

CHAPTER III

I BEGIN MY DUTIES AS TUTOR—THE CZAREVITCH'S ILLNESS
(AUTUMN, 1913)

CHAPTER III

I BEGIN MY DUTIES AS TUTOR—THE CZAREVITCH'S ILLNESS (AUTUMN, 1913)

I RETURNED to St. Petersburg at the end of August. The Imperial family was in the Crimea. I called on the Controller of Her Majesty's Household for my instructions and left for Livadia, which I reached on September 3rd. I found Alexis Nicolaïevitch pale and thin. He still suffered very much, and was undergoing a course of high-temperature mud-baths, which the doctors had ordered as a cure for the last traces of his accident but which he found extremely trying.

Naturally I waited to be summoned by the Czarina to receive exact instructions and suggestions from her personally. But she did not appear at meals and was not to be seen. She merely informed me through Tatiana Nicolaïevna that while the treatment was in progress regular lessons with Alexis Nicolaïevitch were out of the question. As she wished the boy to get used to me, she asked me to go with him on his walks and spend as much time with him as I could.

I then had a long talk with Dr. Derevenko. He told me that the Heir was a prey to hæmophilia, a hereditary disease which in certain families is transmitted from generation to generation *by the women* to their male children. Only males are affected. He told me that the slightest wound might cause the boy's death, for the blood of a bleeder had not the power of coagulating like that of a normal individual. Further, the tissue of the arteries and veins is so frail that any blow or shock may rupture the blood-vessel and bring on a fatal hæmorrhage.

Such was the terrible disease from which Alexis Nicolaïevitch was suffering, such the perpetual menace to his life. A fall, nose-bleeding, a simple cut—things which were a trifle to any other child—might prove fatal to him. All that could be done was to watch over him closely day and night, especially in his early years,[1] and by extreme vigilance try to prevent accidents. Hence the fact that at the suggestion of the doctors he had been given two ex-sailors of the Imperial yacht, Derevenko and his assistant Nagorny, as his personal attendants and bodyguard. They looked after him in rotation.

My first relations with the boy in my new appointment were not easy. I was obliged to talk in Russian with him and give up French. My position was delicate, as I had no rights and therefore no hold over him.

As I have said, at first I was astonished and disappointed at the lack of support given me by the Czarina. A whole month had passed before I received any instructions from her. I had a feeling that she did not want to come between her son and myself. It made my initial task much more difficult, but it might have the advantage, once I had established my position, of enjoying it with greater freedom and personal

---

[1] About 85 per cent. of bleeders die in their childhood or early youth. The chances of a fatal issue diminish greatly as they attain manhood. That is easily understood. An adult knows how to exercise the care his condition requires, and the causes of trauma are thus greatly lessened. Although hæmophilia is incurable, it does not prevent many of its victims from reaching an advanced old age. The children of Alexis Nicolaïevitch would not have been affected by this terrible malady, as it is only transmitted by women.

authority.   About this time I had moments of extreme dis-
couragement, and in fact I sometimes despaired of success and
felt ready to abandon the task I had undertaken.

Fortunately for me, in Dr. Derevenko I found a wise
adviser whose help was of infinite value.   He impressed on me
the necessity for patience, and told me that, in view of the
constant danger of the boy's relapse, and as a result of a kind of
religious fatalism which the Czarina had developed, she tended
to leave decision to circumstance and kept on postponing her
intervention, which would simply inflict useless suffering on her
son if he was not to survive.   She did not feel equal to battling
with the child to make him accept me.

I understood myself, of course, that circumstances were
unfavourable, but I still cherished a hope that one day the
health of my pupil would improve.

The serious malady from which the Czarevitch had barely
recovered had left him very weak and nervous.   At this time
he was the kind of child who can hardly bear correction.   He
had never been under any regular discipline.   In his eyes I was
the person appointed to extract work and attention from him,
and it was my business to bend his will to the habit of obedience.
To all the existing supervision, which at any rate allowed him
idleness as a place of refuge, was to be added a new control
which would violate even that last retreat.   He felt it instinc-
tively without realising it consciously.   I had a definite impression of his mute hostility, and at times it reached a stage of
open defiance.

I felt a terrible burden of responsibility, for with all my
precautions it was impossible always to prevent accidents.
There were three in the course of the first month.

Yet as time passed by I felt my authority gaining a hold.

I noticed more and more frequent bursts of confidence on the part of my pupil, and they seemed to me a promise of affectionate relations before long.

The more the boy opened his heart to me the better I realised the treasures of his nature, and I gradually began to feel certain that with so many precious gifts it would be unjust to give up hope.

Alexis Nicolaïevitch was then nine and a half, and rather tall for his age. He had a long, finely-chiselled face, delicate features, auburn hair with a coppery glint in it, and large blue-grey eyes like his mother's. He thoroughly enjoyed life —when it let him—and was a happy, romping boy. Very simple in his tastes, he extracted no false satisfaction from the fact that he was the Heir—there was nothing he thought about less—and his greatest delight was to play with the two sons of his sailor Derevenko, both of them a little younger than he.

He had very quick wits and a keen and penetrating mind. He sometimes surprised me with questions beyond his years which bore witness to a delicate and intuitive spirit. I had no difficulty in believing that those who were not forced, as I was, to teach him habits of discipline, but could unreservedly enjoy his charm, easily fell under its spell. Under the capricious little creature I had known at first I discovered a child of a naturally affectionate disposition, sensitive to suffering in others just because he had already suffered so much himself. When this conviction had taken root in my mind I was full of hope for the future. My task would have been easy had it not been for the Czarevitch's associates and environment.

As I have already said, I was on excellent terms with Dr. Derevenko. There was, however, one point on which we were

THE FOUR GRAND-DUCHESSES GATHERING MUSHROOMS IN THE
/FOREST OF BIELOVESA, AUTUMN OF 1912.

THE CZAREVITCH CUTTING CORN HE HAD SOWN IN THE PARK AT
PETERHOF, SUMMER OF 1913.

[*Facing page* 10.

not in agreement. I considered that the perpetual presence of the sailor Derevenko and his assistant Nagorny was harmful to the child. The external power which intervened whenever danger threatened seemed to me to hinder the development of will-power and the faculty of observation. What the child gained—possibly—in safety he lost in real discipline. I thought it would have been better to give him more freedom and accustom him to look to himself for the energy to resist the impulses of his own motion.

Besides, accidents continued to happen. It was impossible to guard against everything, and the closer the supervision became, the more irritating and humiliating it seemed to the boy, and the greater the risk that it would develop his skill at evasion and make him cunning and deceitful. It was the best way of turning an already physically delicate child into a characterless individual, without self-control and backbone, even in the moral sense.

I spoke in that sense to Dr. Derevenko, but he was so obsessed by fears of a fatal attack, and so conscious of the terrible load of responsibility that devolved upon him as the doctor, that I could not bring him round to share my view.

It was for the parents, and the parents alone, in the last resort, to take a decision which might have serious consequences for their child. To my great astonishment, they entirely agreed with me, and said they were ready to accept all the risks of an experiment on which I did not enter myself without terrible anxiety. No doubt they realised how much harm the existing system was doing to all that was best in their son, and if they loved him to distraction their love itself gave them the strength to let him run the risk of an accident which might prove fatal rather than see him grow up a man without strength of character or moral fibre.

Alexis Nicolaïevitch was delighted at this decision. In his relations with his playmates he was always suffering from the incessant supervision to which he was subject. He promised me to repay the confidence reposed in him.

Yet, sure though I was of the soundness of my view, the moment the parents' consent was obtained my fears were greater than ever. I seemed to have a presentiment of what was to come. . . .

Everything went well at first, and I was beginning to be easy in my mind, when the accident I had so much feared happened without a word of warning. The Czarevitch was in the schoolroom standing on a chair, when he slipped, and in falling hit his right knee against the corner of some piece of furniture. The next day he could not walk. On the day after the subcutaneous hæmorrhage had progressed, and the swelling which had formed below the knee rapidly spread down the leg. The skin, which was greatly distended, had hardened under the force of the extravasated blood, which pressed on the nerves of the leg and thus caused shooting pains, which grew worse every hour.

I was thunderstruck. Yet neither the Czar nor the Czarina blamed me in the slightest. So far from it, they seemed to be intent on preventing me from despairing of a task my pupil's malady made so perilous. As if they wished by their example to make me face the inevitable ordeal, and enlist me as an ally in the struggle they had carried on so long, they associated me in their anxieties with a truly touching kindness.

The Czarina was at her son's side from the first onset of the attack. She watched over him, surrounding him with her tender love and care and trying by a thousand attentions to alleviate his sufferings. The Czar came the moment he was free. He tried to comfort and amuse the boy, but the pain was stronger than his mother's caresses or his father's stories, and the moans and tears began once more. Every now and then the door opened and one of the Grand-Duchesses came in on tip-toe and kissed her little brother, bringing a gust of sweetness and health into the room. For a moment the boy would open his great eyes, round which the malady had already painted black rings, and then almost immediately close them again.

One morning I found the mother at her son's bedside. He had had a very bad night. Dr. Derevenko was anxious, as the hæmorrhage had not been stopped and his temperature was rising. The inflammation had spread further and the pain was even worse than the day before. The Czarevitch lay in bed groaning piteously. His head rested on his mother's arm, and his small, deathly-white face was unrecognisable. At times the groans ceased and he murmured the one word " Mummy ! " in which he expressed all his sufferings and distress. His mother kissed him on the hair, forehead, and eyes, as if the touch of her lips could have relieved his pain and restored some of the life which was leaving him. Think of the tortures of that mother, an impotent witness of her son's martyrdom in those hours of mortal anguish—a mother who knew that *she herself* was the cause of his sufferings, that *she* had transmitted to him the terrible disease against which human science was powerless ! *Now* I understood the secret tragedy of her life ! How easy it was to reconstruct the stages of that long Calvary.

CHAPTER IV
THE CZARINA, ALEXANDRA FEODOROVNA

CHAPTER IV

THE CZARINA, ALEXANDRA FEODOROVNA

THE Czarina, Alexandra Feodorovna, formerly Alice of Hesse, and fourth child of the Grand Duke Ludwig of Hesse and Alice of England, youngest daughter of Queen Victoria, was born at Darmstadt on June 6th, 1872. She lost her mother early in life, and was largely brought up at the English Court, where she soon became the favourite granddaughter of Queen Victoria, who bestowed on the blonde " Alix " all the tender affection she had had for her mother.[1]

At the age of seventeen the young princess paid a prolonged visit to Russia, staying with her elder sister Elisabeth, who had married the Grand-Duke Sergius Alexandrovitch, a brother of the Czar Alexander III. She took an active part in Court life, appeared at reviews, receptions, and balls, and being very pretty was made a great fuss of.

Everybody regarded her as the prospective mate of the Heir to the Throne, but, contrary to general expectation, Alice of Hesse returned to Darmstadt and nothing had been said. Did she not like the idea ? It is certainly a fact that five years later, when the official proposal arrived, she showed signs of hesitation.

---

[1] Queen Victoria did not like the Germans and had a particular aversion for the Emperor William II., which she handed on to her granddaughter, who always preferred England, her country on her mother's side, to Germany. Yet she always remained greatly attached to the friends and relations she had left there.

However, the betrothal took place at Darmstadt during the summer of 1894, and was followed by a visit to the Court of England. The Russian Heir at once returned to his country. A few months later she was obliged to leave suddenly for Livadia, where Alexander III. was dying. She was present when his end came, and with the Imperial family accompanied the coffin in which the mortal remains of the dead Emperor were carried to St. Petersburg.

The body was taken from Nicholas station to the Cathedral of St. Peter and St. Paul on a dull November day. A huge crowd was assembled on the route of the funeral cortège as it moved through the melting snow and mud with which the streets were covered. In the crowd women crossed themselves piously and could be heard murmuring, in allusion to the young Czarina, " She has come to us behind a coffin. She brings misfortune with her."

It certainly seemed as if from the start sorrow was dodging the steps of her whose light heart and beauty had earned her the nickname of " Sunshine " in her girlhood.

On November 26th, thus within a month of Alexander's death, the marriage was celebrated amidst the general mourning. A year later the Czarina gave birth to her first child—a daughter who was named Olga.

The coronation of the young sovereigns took place in Moscow on May 14th, 1896. Fate seemed already to have marked them down. It will be remembered that the celebrations were the occasion of a terrible accident which cost the lives of a large number of people. The peasants, who had come from all parts, had assembled in masses during the night in Hodinskoïe meadows, where gifts were to be distributed. As a result of bad organisation there was a panic, and more than two thousand people were trodden to death or suffocated in the mud by the terror-stricken crowd.

When the Czar and Czarina went to Hodinskoïe meadows next morning they had heard nothing whatever of the terrible catastrophe. They were not told the truth until they returned to the city subsequently, and they never knew the whole truth. Did not those concerned realise that by acting thus they were depriving the Imperial couple of a chance to show their grief and sympathy and making their behaviour odious because it seemed sheer indifference to public misfortune ?

Several years of domestic bliss followed, and Fate seemed to have loosened its grip.

Yet the task of the young Czarina was no easy one. She had to learn all that it meant to be an empress, and that at the most etiquette-ridden Court in Europe and the scene of the worst forms of intrigue and coterie. Accustomed to the simple life of Darmstadt, and having experienced at the strict and formal English Court only such restraint as affected a young and popular princess who was there merely on a visit, she must have felt at sea with her new obligations and dazzled by an existence of which all the proportions had suddenly changed. Her sense of duty and her burning desire to devote herself to the welfare of the millions whose Czarina she had become fired her ambitions, but at the same time checked her natural impulses.

Yet her only thought was to win the hearts of her subjects. Unfortunately she did not know how to show it, and the innate timidity from which she suffered was wont to play the traitor to her kind intentions. She very soon realised how impotent she was to gain sympathy and understanding. Her frank and spontaneous nature was speedily repelled by the icy conventions of her environment. Her impulses came up against the prevalent inertia about her, [1] and when in return for her confidence she asked for intelligent devotion and real good will, those with whom she dealt took refuge in the easy zeal of the polite formalities of Courts.

In spite of all her efforts, she never succeeded in being merely amiable and acquiring the art which consists of flitting gracefully but superficially over all manner of subjects. The fact is that the Czarina was nothing if not sincere. Every word from her lips was the true expression of her real feelings. Finding herself misunderstood, she quickly drew back into her shell. Her natural pride was wounded. She appeared less and less at the ceremonies and receptions she regarded as an intolerable nuisance. She adopted a habit of distant reserve which was taken for haughtiness and contempt. But those who came in contact with her in moments of distress knew what a sensitive spirit, what a longing for affection, was concealed behind that apparent coldness. She had accepted her new religion with entire sincerity, and found it a great source of comfort in hours of trouble and anguish ; but above all, it was the affection of her family which nourished her love, and she was never really happy except when she was with them.

The birth of Olga Nicolaïevna had been followed by that of three other fine and healthy daughters who were their parents' delight. It was not an unmixed delight, however, for the secret desire of their hearts—to have a son and heir—had not yet been fulfilled. The birth of Anastasie Nicolaïevna, the

---

[1] She was extremely anxious to improve the lot of poor women by building maternity and other hospitals. She hoped to establish professional schools, and so on.

last of the Grand-Duchesses, had at first been a terrible disappointment . . . and the years were slipping by. At last,
on August 12th, 1904, when the Russo-Japanese War was at
its height, the Czarina gave birth to the son they so ardently
desired. Their joy knew no bounds. It seemed as if all the
sorrows of the past were forgotten and that an era of happiness
was about to open for them.

Alas ! it was but a short respite, and was followed by worse
misfortunes : first the January massacre in front of the Winter
Palace—the memory of which was to haunt them like a horrible
nightmare for the rest of their days—and then the lamentable
conclusion of the Russo-Japanese War. In those dark days
their only consolation was their beloved son, and it had not
taken long, alas ! to discover that the Czarevitch had hæmophilia. From that moment the mother's life was simply one
dreadful agony. She had already made the acquaintance of
that terrible disease ; she knew that an uncle, one of her
brothers, and two of her nephews had died of it. From her
childhood she had heard it spoken of as a dreadful and mysterious thing against which men were powerless. And now her
only son, the child she loved more than anything else on earth,
was affected ! Death would watch him, follow him at every
step, and carry him off one day like so many boys in his family.
She must fight ! She must save him at any cost ! It was
impossible for science to be impotent. The means of saving
must exist, and they must be found. Doctors, surgeons,
specialists were consulted. But every kind of treatment was
tried in vain.

When the mother realised that no human aid could save,
her last hope was in God. He alone could perform the miracle.
But she must be worthy of His intervention. She was naturally

of a pious nature, and she devoted herself wholly to the Orthodox religion with the ardour and determination she brought to everything. Life at Court became strict, if not austere. Festivities were eschewed, and the number of occasions on which the sovereigns had to appear in public was reduced to a minimum. The family gradually became isolated from the Court and lived to itself, so to speak.

Between each of the attacks, however, the boy came back to life, recovered his health, forgot his sufferings, and resumed his fun and his games. At these times it was impossible to credit that he was the victim of an implacable disease which might carry him off at any moment. Every time the Czarina saw him with red cheeks, or heard his merry laugh, or watched his frolics, her heart would fill with an immense hope, and she would say : " God has heard me. He has pitied my sorrow at last." Then the disease would suddenly swoop down on the boy, stretch him once more on his bed of pain and take him to the gates of death.

The months passed, the expected miracle did not happen, and the cruel, ruthless attacks followed hard on each other's heels. The most fervent prayers had not brought the divine revelation so passionately implored. The last hope had failed. A sense of endless despair filled the Czarina's soul : it seemed as if the whole world were deserting her.[1]

It was then that Rasputin, a simple Siberian peasant, was brought to her, and he said : " Believe in the power of my prayers ; believe in my help and your son will live ! "

The mother clung to the hope he gave her as a drowning man seizes an outstretched hand. She believed in him with

---

[1] Her continual fear of an attempt on the life of the Czar or her son always helped to wear down the Czarina's nervous vitality.

all the strength that was in her.   As a matter of fact, she had
been convinced for a long time that the saviour of Russia and
the dynasty would come from the people, and she thought that
this humble *moujik* had been sent by God to save him who was
the hope of the nation.   The intensity of her faith did the rest,
and by a simple process of auto-suggestion, which was helped
by certain perfectly casual coincidences, she persuaded herself
that her son's life was in this man's hands.

Rasputin had realised the state of mind of the despairing
mother who was broken down by the strain of her struggle and
seemed to have touched the limit of human suffering.   He
knew how to extract the fullest advantage from it, and with a
diabolical cunning he succeeded in associating his own life, so
to speak, with that of the child.

This moral hold of Rasputin on the Czarina cannot possibly
be understood unless one is familiar with the part played in the
religious life of the Orthodox world by those men who are
neither priests nor monks—though people habitually, and quite
inaccurately, speak of the " monk " Rasputin—and are called
stranniki or *startsi*.

The *strannik* is a pilgrim who wanders from monastery to
monastery and church to church, seeking the truth and living
on the charity of the faithful.   He may thus travel right across
the Russian Empire, led by his fancy or attracted by the
reputation for holiness enjoyed by particular places or persons.

The *staretz* is an ascetic who usually lives in a monastery,
though sometimes in solitude—a kind of guide of souls to whom
one has recourse in moments of trouble or suffering.   Quite
frequently a *staretz* is an ex-*strannik* who has given up his old
wandering life and taken up an abode in which to end his days
in prayer and meditation.

Dostoïevsky gives the following description of him in *The Brothers Karamazof* :

> " The *staretz* is he who takes your soul and will and makes them his. When you select your *staretz* you surrender your will, you give it him in utter submission, in full renunciation. He who takes this burden upon him, who accepts this terrible school of life, does so of his own free will in the hope that after a long trial he will be able to conquer himself and become his own master sufficiently to attain complete freedom by a life of obedience—that is to say, get rid of self and avoid the fate of those who have lived their lives without succeeding in sufficing unto themselves."

God gives the *staretz* the indications which are requisite for one's welfare and communicates the means by which one must be brought back to safety.

On earth the *staretz* is the guardian of truth and the ideal. He is also the repository of the sacred tradition which must be transmitted from *staretz* to *staretz* until the reign of justice and light shall come.

Several of these *startsi* have risen to remarkable heights of modern grandeur and become saints of the Orthodox Church.

The influence of these men, who live as a kind of unofficial clergy, is still very considerable in Russia. In the provinces and open country it is even greater than that of the priests and monks.

The conversion of the Czarina had been a genuine act of faith. The Orthodox religion had fully responded to her mystical aspirations, and her imagination must have been

captured by its archaic and naïve ritual.   She had accepted it
with all the ardour of the neophyte.   In her eyes Rasputin had
all the prestige and sanctity of a *staretz*.

Such was the nature of the feelings the Czarina entertained
for Rasputin—feelings ignobly travestied by calumny.   They
had their source in maternal love, the noblest passion which
can fill a mother's heart.

Fate willed that he who wore the halo of a saint should be
nothing but a low and perverse creature, and that, as we shall
soon see, this man's evil influence was one of the principal
causes of which the effect was the death of those who thought
they could regard him as their saviour.

CHAPTER V

RASPUTIN

CHAPTER V

RASPUTIN

IN the preceding chapter I thought I ought to dwell on events some of which took place before I took up my duties, because they alone could explain the fundamental reasons why Rasputin was ever able to appear on the scene and obtain so great an influence over the Czarina.

I should have preferred to confine my book to events in which I have taken a direct part and give personal evidence only. But if I did so my story could not be clear. In the present chapter I am compelled once more to depart from the rule I wished to lay down for myself. If the reader is to understand me, it is essential for me to give certain details about the life and beginnings of Rasputin and to try and disentangle from the legends innumerable of which he is the subject such facts as seem to me part of history.

About one hundred and fifty versts south of Tobolsk the little village of Pokrovskoïe lies lost in the marshes on the banks of the Tobol. There Grigory Rasputin was born. His father's name was Efim. Like many other Russian peasants at that time, the latter had no family name. The inhabitants of the village, of which he was not a native, had given him on his arrival the name of Novy (the Newcomer).

His son Grigory had the same kind of youth as all the small peasantry of that part of Siberia, where the poor quality of the soil often compels them to live by expedients.   Like them, he robbed and stole. . . . He soon made his mark, however, by the audacity he showed in his exploits, and it was not long before his misdoings earned him the reputation of an unbridled libertine.   He was now known solely as Rasputin, a corruption of the word *rasputnik* (debauched), which was destined to become, as it were, his family name.

The villagers of Siberia were in the habit of hiring out horses to travellers passing through the country and offering their services as guides and coachmen.   One day Rasputin happened to conduct a priest to the monastery of Verkhoturie.   The priest entered into conversation with him, was struck by his quick natural gifts, led him by his questions to confess his riotous life, and exhorted him to consecrate to the service of God the vitality he was putting to such bad uses.   The exhortation produced so great an impression on Grigory that he seemed willing to give up his life of robbery and licence. He stayed for a considerable time at the monastery of Verkhoturie and began to frequent the holy places of the neighbourhood.

When he went back to his village he seemed a changed man, and the inhabitants could hardly recognise the reprobate hero of so many scandalous adventures in this man whose countenance was so grave and whose dress so austere.   He was seen going from village to village, spreading the good word and reciting to all and sundry willing to listen long passages from the sacred books, which he knew by heart.

Public credulity, which he already exploited extremely skilfully, was not slow in regarding him as a prophet, a being endowed with supernatural powers, and in particular the power of performing miracles.   To understand this rapid transforma-

Si vous avez le second volume de „Notre Dame de Paris" envoyez le moi je vous en prie.

Olga Romanoff

13 - May 1914

LETTER TO THE AUTHOR FROM THE GRAND-DUCHESS OLGA NICOLAÏEVNA
(LIVADIA, CRIMEA, MAY 13/26, 1914).

[Facing page 60.

tion one must realise both the strange power of fascination and suggestion which Rasputin possessed, and also the ease with which the popular imagination in Russia is captured by the attraction of the marvellous.

However, the virtue of the new saint does not seem to have been proof against the enticements of the flesh for long, and he relapsed into his debauchery. It is true that he showed the greatest contrition for his wrongdoings, but that did not prevent him from continuing them. Even at that time he displayed that blend of mysticism and erotomania which made him so dangerous a person.

Yet, notwithstanding all this, his reputation spread far and wide. His services were requisitioned, and he was sent for from distant places, not merely in Siberia, but even in Russia.

His wanderings at last brought him to St. Petersburg. There, in 1905, he made the acquaintance of the Archimandrite Theophanes, who thought he could discern in him signs of genuine piety and profound humility as well as the marks of divine inspiration. Rasputin was introduced by him to devout circles in the capital, whither his reputation had preceded him. He had no difficulty in trafficking in the credulity of these devotees, whose very refinement made them superstitious and susceptible to the magnetism of his rustic piety In his fundamental coarseness they saw nothing but the entertaining candour of a man of the people. They were filled with the greatest admiration for the *naïveté* of this simple soul. . . .

It was not long before Rasputin had immense authority with his new flock. He became a familiar figure in the *salons* of certain members of the high aristocracy of St. Petersburg, and was even received by members of the royal family, who sang his praises to the Czarina. Nothing more was requisite for the last and vital stage. Rasputin was taken to Court by intimate friends of Her Majesty, and with a personal recommendation from the Archimandrite Theophanes. This last fact must always be borne in mind. It was to shelter him from the attacks of his enemies for many years.

We have seen how Rasputin traded on the despair which possessed the Czarina and had contrived to link his life with that of the Czarevitch and acquire a growing hold over his mother. Each of his appearances seemed to produce an improvement in the boy's malady, and thus increased his prestige and confirmed confidence in the power of his intercession.

After a certain time, however, Rasputin's head was turned by this unexpected rise to fame ; he thought his position was sufficiently secure, forgot the caution he had displayed when he first came to St. Petersburg, and returned to his scandalous mode of life. Yet he did so with a skill which for a long time kept his private life quite secret. It was only gradually that the reports of his excesses spread and were credited.

At first only a few voices were faintly raised against the *staretz*, but it was not long before they became loud and numerous. The first at Court to attempt to show up the impostor was Mademoiselle Tioutcheva, the governess of the Grand-Duchesses. Her efforts were broken against the blind faith of the Czarina. Among the charges she made against Rasputin were several which, in her indignation, she had not checked with sufficient care so that their falsity was absolutely patent to her sovereign. Realising her impotence, and with a view to discharging her responsibilities, she asked that in any case Rasputin should not be allowed on the floor occupied by the children.

The Czar then intervened, and Her Majesty yielded, not because her faith was shaken, but merely for the sake of peace and in the interests of a man whom she believed was blinded by his very zeal and devotion.

Although I was then no more than one of the Grand-Duchesses' professors—it was during the winter of 1910—Mademoiselle Tioutcheva herself told me all about this debate and its vicissitudes.[1] But I confess that at that time I was still far from accepting all the extraordinary stories about Rasputin.

In March, 1911, the hostility to Rasputin became more and more formidable, and the *staretz* thought it wise to let the storm blow over and disappear for a time. He therefore started on a pilgrimage to Jerusalem.

On his return to St. Petersburg in the autumn of the same year the tumult had not subsided, and he had to face the attacks of one of his former protectors, Bishop Hermogenes, who employed terrible threats and eventually extracted a promise from Rasputin to keep away from the Court, where his presence compromised his sovereigns.

He had no sooner left the Bishop, who had actually gone so far as to strike him, than he rushed to his powerful protectress, Madame Wyroubova, the Czarina's all but inseparable companion. The Bishop was exiled to a monastery.

Just as futile were the efforts of the Archimandrite Theophanes, who could never forgive himself for having stood sponsor in some degree for the *staretz's* high moral character,

---

[1] Relations between the Czarina and Mlle. Tioutcheva were never again what they had been, and the latter resigned her post in the spring of 1912.

and thus reassuring the Czar and Czarina by his personal recommendation. He did his best to show him up, but the only reward for his pains was to find himself transferred to the Government of Tauris.

The fact was that Rasputin managed to make the two Bishops seem low intriguers who had wanted to use him as an instrument, and then, becoming jealous of a favour they could no longer exploit for their own personal benefit, tried to bring about his downfall.

" The lowly Siberian peasant " had become a formidable adversary in whom an utter lack of moral scruple was associated with consummate skill. With a first-class intelligence service, and creatures of his own both at Court and among the men around the ministers, as soon as he saw a new enemy appear on the scene he was always careful to baulk him cleverly by getting in the first blow.

Under the form of prophecies he would announce that he was going to be the object of a new attack, taking good care not to indicate his adversaries too plainly. So when the bolt was shot, the hand that directed it held a crumbling missile. He often actually interceded in favour of those who had attacked him, affirming with mock humility that such trials were necessary for the good of his soul.

Another element which also contributed to keep alive the blind faith in him which lasted until the end was the fact that the Czar and Czarina were accustomed to see those to whom they paid particular attention become objects of intrigue and cabals. They knew that their esteem alone was sufficient to expose them to the attacks of the envious. The result was that they were convinced that the special favour they showed to an obscure *moujik* was bound in any case to raise a storm of hate and jealousy against him and make him the victim of the worst calumnies.

The scandal, however, gradually spread from the purely ecclesiastical world. It was mentioned in whispers in political and diplomatic circles, and was even referred to in speeches in the Duma.

In the spring of 1912, Count Kokovtzof, then President of the Council of Ministers, decided to take the matter up with the Czar. The step was a particularly delicate one, as hitherto Rasputin's influence had been confined to the Church and the Imperial family circle. Those were the very spheres in which the Czar was most intolerant of any interference by his ministers.

The Czar was not convinced by the Count's action, but he realised that some concession to public opinion was necessary. Shortly after Their Majesties went to the Crimea, Rasputin left St. Petersburg and vanished into Siberia.

Yet his influence was of the kind that distance does not diminish. On the contrary, it only idealised him and increased his prestige.

As in his previous absences, there was a lively exchange of telegrams—through the medium of Madame Wyroubova—between Pokrovskoïe and the different residences occupied in turn by the Imperial family during the year 1912.

The absent Rasputin was more powerful than Rasputin in the flesh. His psychic empire was based on an act of faith, for there is no limit to the power of self-delusion possessed by those who mean to believe at all cost. The history of mankind is there to prove it !

But how much suffering and what terrible disasters were to result from the tragic aberration !

E

CHAPTER VI

LIFE AT TSARSKOÏE-SELO—MY PUPILS
(THE WINTER OF 1913-14)

CHAPTER VI

LIFE AT TSARSKOÏE-SELO—MY PUPILS (THE WINTER OF 1913-14)

TO Rasputin was once more attributed the improvement in Alexis Nicolaïevitch's health a few days after the terrible attack to which I have referred.

It will be remembered that the attack had occurred shortly after that change in the Czarevitch's manner of life I had thought it my duty to advocate. I thus felt partially responsible.

I was in a very great difficulty. When I decided as I did, I had, of course, realised the great dangers involved and thought myself strong enough to face them. But the test of reality was so dreadful that I had to consider whether I ought to persevere. . . . And yet I felt strongly that I had no alternative.

After two months' convalescence—the Czarevitch only recovered slowly—the Czar and Czarina made up their minds to persevere with the method they had adopted, notwithstanding the risks.

Dr. Botkin[1] and Dr. Derevenko were of a contrary opinion, but bowed to the parents' desires and bravely accepted a decision which added considerably to the difficulties of a task

---

Son of the famous Professor Sergius Botkin and Court Physician.

which was exacting and unpromising enough as it was.   They were always on the look-out for the possible crisis, and when the accident happened the struggle was all the harder for them because they realised the inadequacy of the remedies at their disposal.   When, after nights of watching, they had the joy of seeing their young patient out of danger, the improvement was attributed, not to their care and efforts, but to the miraculous intervention of Rasputin !   But there was no false pride or envy about them, for they were inspired by feelings of the deepest pity for the tortured mother and father and the sufferings of the child who, at ten years of age, had already had far more to bear than most men in a long lifetime.

Our stay in the Crimea was longer than usual owing to Alexis Nicolaïevitch's illness, and we only returned to Tsarskoïe-Selo in December.   We then spent the whole winter of 1913-14 there.

Our life at Tsarskoïe-Selo was far more intimate than when we were in residence at other palaces.   With the exception of the maid-of-honour on duty and the officer commanding the " composite " [1] regiment, the suite did not live in the palace, and unless relations were visiting the family the latter generally took their meals alone very quietly.

Lessons [2] began at nine o'clock, and there was a break from eleven to twelve.   We went out driving in a carriage, sledge, or car, and then work was resumed until lunch at one.   In the afternoon we always spent two hours out of doors.   The Grand-Duchesses and, when he was free, the Czar, came with us, and Alexis Nicolaïevitch played with them, sliding on an ice

---

[1] The regiment which acted as the Czar's bodyguard.   It comprised representatives of all the regiments of the Guard.

[2] At the time my pupil was learning Russian, French, arithmetic, history, geography and religious knowledge.   He did not begin English until later, and never had German lessons.

THE CZAREVITCH WITH HIS DOG "JOY" ON THE BALCONY OF THE
ALEXANDER PALACE, TSARSKOÏE-SELO. SEPTEMBER, 1914.

[*Facing page* 70.

mountain we had made at the edge of a little artificial lake. He was also fond of playing with his donkey Vanka, which was harnessed to a sledge, and his dog Joy, an attractive little liver spaniel with short legs, and long silky ears which almost touched the ground.

Vanka was a creature of quite unusual intelligence and sense of humour. When the idea of giving Alexis Nicolaïevitch a donkey had been mooted, all the horse-dealers in St. Petersburg had been referred to in vain. Cinizelli's Circus had then agreed to part with a thoroughbred animal which had grown too old to perform any longer. Thus had Vanka come to Court, and he seemed to be immensely attached to the young family. He certainly was most amusing, for his repertoire of tricks was quite inexhaustible. In the most expert manner imaginable he would turn out your pockets in the hope of discovering delicacies. He was particularly fond of old indiarubber balls, which he would quietly chew, closing one eye like an old Yankee.

These two animals played a large part in the life of Alexis Nicolaïevitch, for his amusements were few. Above all, he was very short of playmates. The two sons of his sailor Derevenko, his ordinary companions, were much younger than he, and had neither the education nor the development desirable.

It is true that his cousins sometimes spent Sundays and birthdays with him, but these visits were rare. I often pressed the Czarina to remedy this state of things. As a result of this pressure an attempt was made, but without result.

Of course, the disease to which the boy was a prey made the choice of his comrades an extremely difficult matter. It was lucky that, as I have said, his sisters liked playing with him. They brought into his life an element of youthful merriment which would otherwise have been sorely missed.

During our afternoon walks, the Czar, who was very fond of walking, usually went round the park with one of his daughters, but quite frequently he came and joined us. It was with his help that we made a huge tower of snow which became quite an imposing fortress before long and kept us busy several weeks.   ›

At four o'clock we went in and resumed lessons until dinner, which was at seven for Alexis Nicolaïevitch and at eight for the rest of the family. We ended the day by reading one of his favourite books.

Alexis Nicolaïevitch was the centre of this united family, the focus of all its hopes and affections. His sisters worshipped him and he was his parents' pride and joy. When he was well the palace was, as it were, transformed. Everyone and everything seemed bathed in sunshine. Endowed with a naturally happy disposition, he would have developed quite regularly and successfully had he not been kept back by his infirmity. Each of his crises meant weeks and sometimes months of the closest attention, and when the hæmorrhage had been heavy it was followed by a condition of general anæmia which made all hard work impossible for him, sometimes for a considerable period. Thus the interludes between attacks were all that were available, and, in spite of his quick brain, this made teaching a difficult matter.

The Grand-Duchesses were charming—the picture of freshness and health. It would have been difficult to find four sisters with characters more dissimilar and yet so perfectly blended in an affection which did not exclude personal independence, and, in spite of contrasting temperaments, kept them a most united family. With the initials of their Christian names they had formed a composite Christian name, Otma, and under this common signature they frequently gave their presents or sent letters written by one of them on behalf of all.

I am sure I shall be forgiven for allowing myself the pleasure of recording some personal memories here—memories which will enable me to recall these girls in all the bloom and spontaneous enthusiasms of their youth. I might almost say their childhood. For these were girls who fell victims to a dreadful fate at a time when others are blossoming into womanhood.

The eldest, Olga Nicolaïevna, possessed a remarkably quick brain. She had good reasoning powers as well as initiative, a very independent manner, and a gift for swift and entertaining repartee. She gave me a certain amount of trouble at first, but our early skirmishes were soon succeeded by relations of frank cordiality.

She picked up everything extremely quickly, and always managed to give an original turn to what she learned. I well remember how, in one of our first grammar lessons, when I was explaining the formation of the verbs and the use of the auxiliaries, she suddenly interrupted me with :

" I see, monsieur. The auxiliaries are the servants of the verbs. It's only poor ' avoir ' which has to shift for itself."

She read a good deal apart from her lessons. When she grew older, every time I gave her a book I was very careful to indicate by notes in the margin the passages or chapters she was to leave out. I used to give her a summary of these. The reason I put forward was the difficulty of the text or the fact that it was uninteresting.

An omission of mine cost me one of the most unpleasant

moments in my professional career, but, thanks to the Czar's presence of mind, the incident ended better than I could have hoped.

Olga Nicolaïevna was reading " Les Miserables," and had reached the description of the battle of Waterloo. At the beginning of the letter she handed me a list of the words she had not understood, in accordance with our practice. What was my astonishment to see in it the word which is forever associated with the name of the officer who commanded the Guard. I felt certain I had not forgotten my usual precautions. I asked for the book to verify my marginal note, and realised my omission. To avoid a delicate explanation I struck out the wretched word and handed back the list to the Grand-Duchess.

She cried, " Why, you've struck out the word I asked papa about yesterday ! "

I could not have been more thunderstruck if the bolt had fallen at my feet.

" What !   You asked your—— "

" Yes, and he asked me how I'd heard of it, and then said it was a very strong word which must not be repeated, though in the mouth of that general it was the finest word in the French language."

A few hours later I met the Czar when I was out walking in the park.   He took me on one side and said in a very serious tone :

" You are teaching my daughters a very curious vocabulary, monsieur. . . ."

I floundered in a most involved explanation.   But the Czar burst out laughing, and interrupted :

" Don't worry, monsieur.   I quite realised what happened,

THE CZARINA AND THE CZAREVITCH IN THE COURT OF THE PALACE AT
LIVADIA. AUTUMN, 1913.

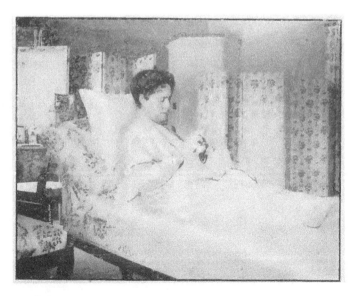

THE CZARINA SEWING IN THE GRAND-DUCHESSES' ROOM.

[Facing page 74.

so I told my daughter that the word was one of the French army's greatest claims to fame."

Tatiana Nicolaïevna was rather reserved, essentially well balanced, and had a will of her own, though she was less frank and spontaneous than her elder sister. She was not so gifted, either, but this inferiority was compensated by more perseverance and balance. She was very pretty, though she had not quite Olga Nicolaïevna's charm.

If the Czarina made any difference between her children, Tatiana Nicolaïevna was her favourite. It was not that her sisters loved their mother any less, but Tatiana knew how to surround her with unwearying attentions and never gave way to her own capricious impulses. Through her good looks and her art of self-assertion she put her sister in the shade in public, as the latter, thoughtless about herself, seemed to take a back seat. Yet the two sisters were passionately devoted to each other. There was only eighteen months between them, and that in itself was a bond of union. They were called " the big pair," while Marie Nicolaïevna and Anastasie Nicolaïevna were still known as the " little pair."

Marie Nicolaïevna was a fine girl, tall for her age, and a picture of glowing health and colour. She had large and beautiful grey eyes. Her tastes were very simple, and with her warm heart she was kindness itself. Her sisters took advantage somewhat of her good nature, and called her " fat little bow-wow." She certainly had the benevolent and somewhat *gauche* devotion of a dog.

Anastasie Nicolaïevna, on the other hand, was very roguish and almost a wag. She had a very strong sense of humour, and the darts of her wit often found sensitive spots. She was rather an *enfant terrible*, though this fault tended to correct itself with age. She was also extremely idle, though with the idleness of a gifted child. Her French accent was excellent, and she acted scenes from comedy with remarkable talent. She was so lively, and her gaiety so infectious, that several members of the suite had fallen into the way of calling her " Sunshine," the nickname her mother had been given at the English Court.

In short, the whole charm, difficult though it was to define, of these four sisters was their extreme simplicity, candour, freshness, and instinctive kindness of heart.

Their mother, whom they adored, was, so to speak, infallible in their eyes. Olga Nicolaïevna alone showed occasional traces of independence. They surrounded her with every attention. Of their own initiative they had arranged matters in such a way that they could take turns of " duty " with their mother, keeping her company for the day. When the Czarina was ill the result was that the daughter on duty could not go out at all.

Their relations with the Czar were delightful. He was Emperor, father, and friend in one.

Their feelings for him were thus dictated by circumstances, passing from religious veneration to utter frankness and the warmest affection. Was it not he before whom the ministers, the highest dignitaries of the Church, the grand-dukes, and even their mother bowed in reverence, he whose fatherly heart opened so willingly to their sorrows, he who joined so merrily in their youthful amusements, far from the eyes of the indiscreet ?

With the exception of Olga Nicolaïevna, the Grand-Duchesses were very moderate pupils. This was largely due to the fact that, in spite of my repeated suggestions, the Czarina would never have a French governess. No doubt she did not wish anyone to come between herself and her daughters. The result was that though they read French, and liked it, they were never able to speak it fluently.[1]

The Czarina's state of health accounts for the fact that the education of her daughters was to some extent neglected. The illness of Alexis Nicolaïevitch had gradually worn down her powers of resistance. At times of crisis she spared herself nothing and displayed remarkable energy and courage. But, once the danger had passed, Nature resumed her rights, and for weeks she would lie on a sofa quite exhausted by the strain.

Olga Nicolaïevna did not fulfil the hopes I had set upon her. Her fine intellect failed to find the elements necessary to its development. Instead of making progress she began to go back. Her sisters had ever had but little taste for learning, their gifts being of the practical order.

By force of circumstances all four had soon learnt to be self-sufficient and to find their natural good nature their sole resource. Very few girls would have accommodated themselves so easily to a life such as theirs—a life deprived of outside amusements, and with no other source of distraction than those joys of family life which are so despised in these days !

---

[1] Her Majesty talked English with them, the Czar Russian only. The Czarina talked English or French with the members of her suite. She never spoke in Russian (though she spoke it pretty well ultimately) except to those who knew no other language. During the whole period of my residence with the Imperial family I never heard one of them utter a word of German, except when it was inevitable, as at receptions, etc.

CHAPTER VII

THE INFLUENCE OF RASPUTIN—MADAME WYROUBOVA—MY TUTORIAL TROUBLES (WINTER OF 1913)

CHAPTER VII

THE INFLUENCE OF RASPUTIN—MADAME WYROUBOVA—MY TUTORIAL TROUBLES (WINTER OF 1913)

WHILE the illness of Alexis Nicolaïevitch threw such a gloom over the Imperial family, and the influence of Rasputin, a product of their very distress, continued to grow, life at Tsarskoïe-Selo seemed to flow along as smoothly as ever, at any rate to outward appearance.

At that time I still knew very little about the *staretz*, and I was searching everywhere for material on which to base my judgment, for his personality interested me decidedly. But it was anything but easy. The children never mentioned Rasputin's name, and in my presence even avoided the slightest allusion to his existence. I realised that in so doing they were acting on their mother's instructions. The Czarina no doubt feared that as a foreigner and not orthodox I was incapable of understanding the nature of the feelings of herself and her family towards the *staretz*, feelings which made them revere him as a saint. By imposing this duty of silence on my pupils she allowed me to ignore Rasputin, or conveyed to me her desire that I should behave as if I knew nothing about him. She thus deprived me of any chance of taking sides against a man whose very name I realised I did not know.

From another source I had been able to convince myself

that Rasputin played a very insignificant part in the life of the Czarevitch. On several occasions Dr. Derevenko told me the amusing remarks Alexis Nicolaïevitch had made about Rasputin in his presence. The latter tickled his young imagination and piqued his curiosity, but had no influence whatever with him.

As a result of Mlle. Tioutcheva's protest, Rasputin no longer went up to the Grand-Duchesses' floor, and he visited the Czarevitch but seldom.

No doubt the authorities were afraid I might meet him, for the rooms I occupied were adjoining those of my pupil. As I had required his personal attendant to keep me informed of the smallest details of his life, Rasputin could not have seen him without my knowledge.[1]

The children saw Rasputin when he was with their parents, but even at that time his visits were infrequent. Weeks, and sometimes months, passed without his being summoned to Court. It became more and more usual to see him with Madame Wyroubova, who had a little house quite near to the Alexander Palace. The Czar and his heir hardly ever went there, and meetings were always very rare.

As I have already explained, Madame Wyroubova was the intermediary between the Czarina and Rasputin. It was she who sent on to the *staretz* letters addressed to him and brought his replies—usually verbal—to the palace.

Relations between Her Majesty and Madame Wyroubova were very intimate, and hardly a day passed without her visiting her Imperial mistress. The friendship had lasted many years. Madame Wyroubova had married very young. Her

---

[1] It was thus that I learned that from January 1st, 1914, to the day of his death in December, 1916, Rasputin only saw Alexis Nicolaïevitch three times.

husband was a degenerate and an inveterate drunkard, and succeeded in inspiring his young wife with a deep hatred of him. They separated, and Madame Wyroubova endeavoured to find relief and consolation in religion. Her misfortunes were a link with the Czarina, who had suffered so much herself, and yearned to comfort her. The young woman who had had to go through so much won her pity. She became the Czarina's confidante, and the kindness the Czarina showed her made her her lifelong slave.

Madame Wyroubova's temperament was sentimental and mystical, and her boundless affection for the Czarina was a positive danger, because it was uncritical and divorced from all sense of reality.

The Czarina could not resist so fiery and sincere a devotion. Imperious as she was, she wanted her friends to be hers, and hers alone. She only entertained friendships in which she was quite sure of being the dominating partner. Her confidence had to be rewarded by complete self-abandonment. She did not realise that it was rather unwise to encourage demonstrations of that fanatical loyalty.

Madame Wyroubova had the mind of a child, and her unhappy experiences had sharpened her sensibilities without maturing her judgment. Lacking in intellect and discrimination, she was the prey of her impulses. Her opinions on men and affairs were unconsidered but none the less sweeping. A single impression was enough to convince her limited and puerile understanding. She at once classified people, according to the impression they made upon her, as " good " or " bad,"—in other words, " friends " or " enemies."

It was with no eye to personal advantage, but out of a pure affection for the Imperial family and her desire to help them, that Madame Wyroubova tried to keep the Czarina posted as to what was going on, to make her share her likes and dislikes, and through her to influence the course of affairs at Court. But in reality she was the docile and unconscious, but none the less mischievous, tool of a group of unscrupulous individuals who used her in their intrigues. She was incapable either of a political policy or considered aims, and could not even guess what was the game of those who used her in their own interests. Without any strength of will, she was absolutely under the influence of Rasputin and had become his most fervent adherent at Court.[1]

I had not seen the *staretz* since I had been at the palace, when one day I met him in the anteroom as I was preparing to go out. I had time to look well at him as he was taking off his cloak. He was very tall, his face was emaciated, and he had piercing grey-blue eyes under thick bushy eyebrows. His hair was long, and he had a long beard like a peasant. He was wearing a Russian smock of blue silk drawn in at the waist, baggy black trousers, and high boots.

This was our one and only meeting, but it left me with a very uncomfortable feeling. During the few moments in which our looks met I had a distinct impression that I was in the presence of a sinister and evil being.

The months slipped by, however, and I had the pleasure of observing the progress made by my pupil. He had grown fond of me and was trying to respond to the trust I showed in

---

[1] Kerensky's "Extraordinary Commission of Enquiry" established the falsity of the libellous reports about her relations with Rasputin. In this connection see the report of M. Roudnief, one of the members of that Commission: "La vérité sur la famille russe" (Paris, 1920). What he says was confirmed during our captivity at Tsarskoïe-Selo by Colonel Korovitchenko, who will come into this book later on

him. I still had a hard struggle against his laziness, but the feeling that the amount of liberty permitted him depended entirely upon the use he made of it fired his zeal and strengthened his will.

It was fortunate that the winter had been a good one, and there had been no other serious relapse after that at Livadia.

Of course I knew quite well that this was only an interlude, but I noticed that Alexis Nicolaïevitch was making a real effort to control his impulsive and turbulent nature, which had unfortunately caused serious accidents, and I began to wonder whether I should not find his illness, however terrible in other ways, an ally which would gradually compel the boy to become his own master and might refine his character.

It was all a great comfort to me, but I cherished no illusions as to the difficulties of my task. I had never realised so well before how his environment fought against my efforts. I had to struggle against the servile flattery of the servants and the silly adulations of some of the people around him. It always surprised me greatly that Alexis Nicolaïevitch's simple nature had hitherto to a large extent resisted the attraction of the extravagant praise he received.

I remember one occasion when a deputation of peasants from one of the Governments of Central Russia came to bring presents to the Czarevitch. The three men of which it was composed, on an order given by Derevenko in a low voice, dropped on their knees before Alexis Nicolaïevitch to offer him what they had brought. I noticed that the boy was embarrassed and blushed violently, and when we were alone I asked him whether he liked seeing people on their knees before him.

" Oh no, but Derevenko says it *must* be so ! "

" That's absurd ! " I replied.   " Even the Czar doesn't like people to kneel before him.   Why don't you stop Derevenko insisting on it ? "

" I don't know.   I dare not."

I took the matter up with Derevenko, and the boy was delighted to be freed from this irksome formality.

But a more serious element was his isolation and the circumstances under which his education was carried on.   I realised that these were almost inevitable, and that the education of a prince tends to make him an incomplete being who finds himself outside life if only because he has not been subject to the common lot in his youth.   Such teaching as he receives can only be artificial, tendencious, and dogmatic.   It often has the absolute and uncompromising character of a catechism.

There are several reasons : the restricted choice of teachers,   · the fact that their liberty of expression is limited by the conventions of their official life and their regard for the exalted position of their pupil, and, finally, that they have to get through a vast programme in a very few years.   It inevitably means that they have to resort to mere formulæ.   They proceed by assertion, and think less of rousing the spirit of enquiry and analysis and stimulating the faculty of comparison in their pupils than of avoiding everything which might awaken an untimely curiosity and a taste for unofficial lines of study.

Further, a child brought up in such conditions is deprived of something which plays a vital part in the formation of judgment.   He is deprived of the knowledge which is acquired out of the schoolroom, knowledge such as comes from life itself, unhampered contact with other children, the diverse and sometimes conflicting influences of environment, direct observation and simple experience of men and affairs—in a word, everything which in the course of years develops the critical faculty and a sense of reality.

Under such circumstances an individual must be endowed with exceptional gifts to be able to see things as they are, think clearly, and desire the right things.

He is cut off from life. He cannot imagine what is going on behind the wall on which false pictures are painted for his amusement or distraction.

All this made me very anxious, but I knew that it would not fall to my lot to remedy this serious state of affairs, so far as it could be remedied. There was a custom in the Russian Imperial family that when the Heir had reached the age of eleven he should be given a *vospitatiet* (educator), whose office was to direct the training and education of the young prince. The *vospitatiet* was usually a soldier, as the military career seemed the best qualification for this heavy and responsible duty. The post was usually given to a general, an ex-director of some military school. It was a highly coveted post in view of the powers and privileges it conferred, and particularly because of the influence the holder might get over the Heir, an influence which often continued during the early years of his reign.

The selection of the *vospitatiet* was thus a vital matter. The direction which Alexis Nicolaïevitch's education would take depended upon him, and I awaited his appointment with considerable anxiety.

CHAPTER VIII

JOURNEYS TO THE CRIMEA AND RUMANIA —PRESIDENT POINCARÉ'S VISIT—DECLARATION OF WAR BY GERMANY (APRIL-JULY, 1914)

CHAPTER VIII

JOURNEYS TO THE CRIMEA AND RUMANIA —PRESIDENT POINCARÉ'S VISIT—DECLARATION OF WAR BY GERMANY (APRIL-JULY; 1914)

IN the spring of 1914 the Imperial family went to the Crimea, as in preceding years. We arrived at Livadia on April 13th, a bright, sunny day. In fact, we were almost dazzled by the sunshine, which bathed the high, steep cliffs, the little Tartar villages half buried in the bare sides of the mountains, and the staring white mosques which stood out sharply against the old cypresses in the cemeteries. The contrast with the landscapes we had just left was so striking that, although this new country was familiar, it seemed quite fairylike and unreal in its wondrous beauty under this halo of sunshine.

These spring days in the Crimea were a delicious relief after the interminable St. Petersburg winter, and we looked forward to them months before they came.

On the excuse of settling in, we all took holiday the first few days, and used it to enjoy this marvel of nature to the full. Then regular lessons were resumed. My colleague, M. Petroff, accompanied us as before.

Alexis Nicolaïevitch's health had improved in recent months ; he had grown a good deal, and he looked so well that we were all in high spirits.

On May 8th the Czar, wishing to give his son a treat, decided that we should take advantage of a day which promised to be particularly sunny to pay a visit to the " Red Rock." We left in a car, the party comprising the Czar, the Czarevitch, an officer from the *Standard*, and myself. The sailor Derevenko and the cossack on duty followed in another car. We gradually ascended the slopes of the Jaila mountains through beautiful forests of pine-trees, whose enormous trunks rose tall and majestic to the leafy dome above them. We soon reached the end of our journey—a huge rock sheer above the valley, and looking as if it had grown rusty in the course of ages.

The day was so fine that the Czar decided to continue the drive. We descended the northern slopes of the Jaila mountains. There was still plenty of snow about, and Alexis Nicolaïevitch had huge fun sliding on it. He ran round us, skipping about, rolling in the snow and picking himself up, only to fall again a few seconds later. It seemed as if his lively nature and *joie de vivre* had never been displayed to better advantage before. The Czar watched his son's frolics with obvious pleasure. You could see how happy he was to realise that the boy had recovered the health and strength of which he had been deprived so long. Yet he was still haunted by the fear of accidents, and every now and then he intervened to moderate his transports. Although he never so much as referred to the disease to which the Heir was a victim, it caused him perpetual anxiety and concern.

The day drew to a close, and we were quite sorry to have to start back. The Czar was in high spirits during the drive. We had an impression that this holiday devoted to his son had been a tremendous pleasure to him. For a few hours he had escaped from his Imperial duties and the attentions, exquisitely

EXCURSION TO THE "RED ROCK" ON MAY 8TH. (THE CRIMEA, SPRING OF 1914.)

THE FOUR GRAND-DUCHESSES (LEFT TO RIGHT: ANASTASIE, OLGA, TATIANA, AND MARIE). STANDARD, 1914.

polite though they were, of those about him. Thanks to the fact that this little trip had been quite impromptu, he had even dodged the vigilant care of the palace police, a thing he felt was always about him (though this duty was performed in the discreetest possible manner), and hated thoroughly. For once, at any rate, he had been able to live like an ordinary mortal. He seemed rested and relieved.

In ordinary times the Czar did not see much of his children. His work and the demands of Court life prevented him from giving them as much time as he would have wished. He had handed over their bringing-up entirely to the Czarina, and in the short time he spent with them in family intimacy he liked to enjoy their company without restraint and with a mind free from all cares. At such times he wanted to be free of the immense burden of responsibility upon his shoulders. He wanted to be simply the father and forget that he was the Czar.

Nothing of any importance occurred to break the monotony of our life during the following weeks.

About the end of May there were rumours at Court that the Grand-Duchess Olga Nicolaïevna was about to be betrothed to Prince Carol of Rumania.[1] She was then eighteen and a half. The parents on both sides seemed in favour of the match, which was very desirable at that moment on political grounds also. I knew that M. Sazonoff, the Minister for Foreign Affairs, was doing his utmost to bring about the betrothal and that the final arrangements were to be made during a visit which the Russian Imperial family were to pay to Rumania in the immediate future.

One day at the beginning of June when I was alone with Olga Nicolaïevna she suddenly asked me a question with that

---

[1] Now Crown Prince of Rumania.

confident and disingenuous frankness which was all her own and the legacy of the relations which had been established between us when she was quite a little girl :

" Tell me the truth, monsieur : do you know why we are going to Rumania ? "

In some confusion I replied :

" I believe it's a courtesy visit.   The Czar is going to return the visit the King of Rumania paid him some time back."

" Oh, that's the official reason . . . but what's the real reason ?   I know you are not supposed to know, but I'm sure everyone is talking about it and that you know it. . . ."

As I nodded in assent, she added :

" All right !   But if I don't wish it, it won't happen. Papa has promised not to make me . . . and I don't want to leave Russia."

" But you could come back as often as you like."

" I should still be a foreigner in my own country.   I'm a Russian, and mean to remain a Russian ! "

On June 13th we embarked on the Imperial yacht *Standard* at Yalta, and the next morning we arrived at Constanza, the great Rumanian port on the Black Sea where the celebrations were to take place.   On the quay a company of infantry with its colours and band received us with military honours, while a battery of artillery posted on the hill above the fort gave us the prescribed salute.   All the ships in the harbour had their flags out.

Their Majesties were received by the old King Carol, Queen Elizabeth ("Carmen Sylva"), and the princes and princesses of the royal family.   After the customary presentations we went to the Cathedral, where a *Te Deum* was celebrated by the Bishop of the Lower Danube.   At one o'clock the members of the two families took luncheon together privately, while the suite were the guests of the President of the Council of Ministers. The royal luncheon was served in the pavilion which " Carmen Sylva " had had built at the pierhead. It was one of her favourite residences, and she spent a considerable part of every year there. She was fond of sitting for hours, "listening to the sea," on the terrace which seemed suspended between the sky and the waves, where the great sea-birds only could break in on her solitude.

In the afternoon Their Majesties gave an At Home on board the *Standard* and then attended a great review.

At eight o'clock in the evening we all assembled for the gala banquet, which was served in a beautiful room built for the purpose. It was certainly charmingly decorated, with its ceiling and walls of white stucco sown with little electric lamps most tastefully disposed and its palms and plants and profusion of well-arranged flowers. The whole thing was a blend of colour and line which was highly pleasing to the eye.

The Czar, with Queen Elizabeth on one side and Princess Marie [1] on the other, was in the centre of a long table at which eighty-four guests were seated. The Czarina sat opposite him, between King Carol and Prince Ferdinand.[2] Olga Nicolaïevna was next to Prince Carol, and replied with her usual natural charm to his questions. The three other Grand-Duchesses, who found it none too easy to conceal their boredom on such occasions, lost no chances of leaning towards me and indicating their sister with a sly wink.

Towards the end of the meal, which proceeded with the usual ceremonial, the King rose to give the Czar a toast of

---

[1] Now Queen of Rumania.　　　[2] Now King of Rumania.

welcome. He spoke in French, but with a strong German accent. The Czar replied, also in French. He spoke pleasantly, in a musical, well-modulated voice. When dinner was over we went into another room, where Their Majesties went round talking to the guests, and those to whom this favour was not accorded lost no time in collecting in groups as affinity or mere chance dictated. But the evening was cut short, as the *Standard* had to leave Constanza the same day. An hour later the yacht put to sea and set sail for Odessa.

The next day I heard that the scheme for the marriage had been abandoned, or at any rate indefinitely postponed. Olga Nicolaïevna had won.[1]

On the morning of June 15th we arrived at Odessa. The Czar reviewed the troops of the garrison, who were presented to him by General Ivanoff, commanding this military area.

The next day we stopped for several hours at Kishineff in Bessarabia in order to be present at the unveiling of a monument to the memory of Alexander I., and on the 18th we returned to Tsarskoïe-Selo. Two days later the Czar was visited by the King of Saxony, who came to thank him for his appointment as honorary colonel of one of the regiments of his Guard. During the visit the troops paraded before the palace. It was the only ceremony which marked the King's short stay On June 23rd he bade farewell to the Imperial family.[2]

Shortly afterwards we left for Peterhof, where we embarked on July 14th for a short cruise in the fjords of Finland. The

---

[1] Who could have foreseen that if the marriage had taken place she would have escaped the dreadful fate in store for her !

[2] A few weeks later the King of Saxony was the only prince in the German Confederation—with the exception of the Grand-Duke of Hesse, the Czarina's brother—who tried to prevent a rupture with Russia. He was averse to associating himself with any employment of force against a nation whose guest he had just been. Yet it did not prevent him from indulging in the most fiery speeches once war had been declared.

Alexandria [1] took us from Peterhof to Cronstadt, where the *Standard* was waiting for us. As we were going on board the Czarevitch jumped at the wrong moment, and his ankle caught the bottom of the ladder leading to the deck. At first I thought this accident would have no ill effects, but towards evening the boy began to be in pain and his sufferings rapidly increased. Everything pointed to a serious crisis.

When I woke next morning we were in the heart of a Finnish fjord. It was an exquisite spot. The sea was deep emerald green, flaked with white by the waves, and dotted with small islands of red granite crowned with pines whose trunks flashed in the sunshine. In the middle distance was the shore, with its long fringe of yellow sand and its dark green forests which stretched away to the horizon.

I went down to Alexis Nicolaïevitch's room. He had had a very bad night. The Czarina and Dr. Botkin were with him, but quite powerless to alleviate his terrible sufferings. [2]

The day passed sullenly and slowly. Since the previous evening I had noticed that the suite were a prey to unwonted excitement. I asked Colonel D—— what the cause was, and learned that there had been an attack on Rasputin and that his life was in danger. He had gone to Siberia a fortnight before, and on his arrival at his own village, Pokrovskoïe, had been stabbed in the stomach by a young women. The wound might be fatal. There was great excitement on board, whisperings and mysterious confabulations which suddenly stopped whenever anyone suspected of being an adherent of Rasputin came near. Everyone else was inspired by a lively hope of

---

[1] A small steam-yacht with paddles. The draught of the *Standard* was too great to allow her to fetch us from Peterhof.
[2] This subcutaneous hæmorrhage is particularly painful when it occurs in a joint.

being at last delivered from that baneful influence, but no one dare reveal his joy too openly. The villainous *moujik* seemed to have nine lives, and he might recover.[1]

On the 19th we returned to Peterhof, where the President of the French Republic was expected. Our cruise was only interrupted, and we were to resume our voyage after he left. Alexis Nicolaïevitch had taken a turn for the better in the last two days, but he was still unable to walk, and he had to be carried off the yacht.

In the afternoon of the next day the cruiser *La France* arrived in Cronstadt harbour with the French President on board. The Czar was there to receive him. They returned to Peterhof together, and M. Poincaré was taken to the apartments prepared for him in the palace. In the evening a gala banquet was given in his honour, and the Czarina and the ladies-in-waiting were present.

For four days the President of the French Republic was the guest of Nicholas II., and many ceremonies marked his short visit. He made an excellent impression upon the Czar, a fact which I was able to prove to my own satisfaction under the following circumstances.

M. Poincaré had been invited to the Imperial luncheon-table, where he was the sole guest. He was received without the slightest formality into the family circle at the little Alexandria Cottage.

When the meal was over the Czarevitch came and showed me, not without considerable pride, the ribbon of the Legion of

---

[1] Rasputin was taken to the hospital at Tioumen and operated upon by a specialist sent from St. Petersburg. The operation was a wonderful success, and a week later the patient was out of danger. His recovery was considered miraculous. Neither fire not steel could avail against one who was obviously under the direct protection of the Almighty!

Honour which the President of the Republic had just given him. We then went out into the park, and in a few minutes we were joined by the Czar.

" Do you know, I've just been talking to M. Poincaré about you ? " he said in his usual affable manner. " He had spoken to Alexis and asked me who had taught him French. He is a remarkable man, with a splendid intellect, and a brilliant talker. That's always useful; but what I like most is that there is nothing of the diplomat about him.[1] He is not reticent, but plain-spoken and frank, and wins one's confidence at once. If only we could do without diplomacy humanity would make immense strides."

On July 23rd the President left Cronstadt for Stockholm, immediately after a dinner given in Their Majesties' honour on the *La France.*

The next day, to our utter amazement, we learned that Austria had presented an ultimatum to Serbia on the previous evening.[2] I met the Czar in the park in the afternoon. He was preoccupied, but did not seem anxious.

On the 25th an Extraordinary Council was held at Krasnoïe-Selo in the Czar's presence. It was decided to pursue a policy of dignified but firm conciliation. The Press was extremely angry at the step taken by Austria.

The next few days the tone of the Press became increasingly violent. Austria was accused of desiring to annihilate Serbia. Russia could not let the little Slav state be overwhelmed.

---

[1] The Czar used to say that diplomacy is the art of making white appear black. *Apropos* of this subject, he once quoted me Bismarck's definition of an ambassador, " A man sent to another country to tell lies for the benefit of his own," and he added : " Thank Heaven they're not all trained in *his* school, but diplomats have a gift for complicating the most simple questions."

[2] Austria delayed the issue of the ultimatum until it was a practical impossibility for news of it to reach St. Petersburg before M. Poincaré left.

She could not tolerate an Austro-Hungarian supremacy in the Balkans. The national honour was at stake.

Yet while tempers were rising and the diplomats were setting the machinery of all the chancelleries in motion, heart-rending telegrams left Alexandria Cottage for distant Siberia, where Rasputin was slowly recovering from his wound in the hospital at Tioumen.[1] They were nearly all of the same tenor : " We are horrified at the prospect of war. Do you think it is possible ? Pray for us. Help us with your counsel."

Rasputin would reply that war must be avoided at any cost if the worst calamities were not to overtake the dynasty and the Empire.

This advice was consonant with the dearest wish of the Czar, whose pacific intentions could not be doubted for a moment. We had only to see him during that terrible last week of July to realise what mental and moral torture he had passed through. But the moment had come when the ambition and perfidy of Germany were to steel him against his own last hesitation and sweep everything with them into the whirlpool.

In spite of all the offers of mediation and the fact that the Russian Government had suggested closing the incident by direct negotiations between St. Petersburg and Vienna, we learned on July 29th that general mobilisation had been ordered in Austria. The next day we heard of the bombardment of Belgrade, and on the following day Russia replied with the mobilisation of her whole army. In the evening of that day Count Pourtalès, the German Ambassador at St. Petersburg, called to inform M. Sazonoff that his Government would give

---

[1] In the winter of 1918, when I was at Tioumen, I saw copies of these very telegrams. Later on I found it impossible to get hold of the text again.

Russia twelve hours in which to stop her mobilisation, failing which Germany would mobilise in turn.[1]

The twelve hours granted to Russia in the ultimatum expired at noon on Saturday, August 1st. Count Pourtalès, however, did not appear at the Ministry for Foreign Affairs until the evening. He was shown in to Sazonoff, and then formally handed him Germany's declaration of war on Russia. It was ten minutes past seven. The irreparable step had been taken.

---

[1] The German General Staff knew only too well that in view of the extreme complexity of the Russian mobilisation (the immense size of the country, the poor railways, etc.), it could not be countermanded without such a disorganisation of the services as would prevent it being resumed for three weeks. A start of three weeks for Germany meant certain victory.

CHAPTER IX

THE IMPERIAL FAMILY IN THE FIRST DAYS OF THE WAR—OUR JOURNEY TO MOSCOW (AUGUST, 1914)

CHAPTER IX

THE IMPERIAL FAMILY IN THE FIRST DAYS OF THE WAR—OUR JOURNEY TO MOSCOW (AUGUST, 1914)

AT the moment when this historic scene was taking place in the Foreign Minister's room at St. Petersburg, the Czar, the Czarina, and their daughters were attending evensong in the little Alexandria church. I had met the Czar a few hours before, and been much struck by the air of weary exhaustion he wore. The pouches which always appeared under his eyes when he was tired seemed to be markedly larger. He was now praying with all the fervour of his nature that God would avert the war which he felt was imminent and all but inevitable.

His whole being seemed to go out in an expression of simple and confident faith. At his side was the Czarina, whose careworn face wore that look of suffering I had so often seen at her son's bedside. She too was praying fervently that night, as if she wished to banish an evil dream. . . .

When the service was over Their Majesties and the Grand-Duchesses returned to Alexandria Cottage. It was almost eight o'clock. Before the Czar came down to dinner he went into his study to read the dispatches which had been brought in his absence. It was thus, from a message from Sazonoff, that he learned of Germany's declaration of war.

He spoke to his Minister on the telephone for a short time and asked him to come down to Alexandria Cottage the moment he could get away.

Meanwhile the Czarina and the Grand-Duchesses were waiting for him in the dining-room. Her Majesty, becoming uneasy at the long delay, had just asked Tatiana Nicolaïevna to fetch her father, when the Czar appeared, looking very pale, and told them that war was declared, in a voice which betrayed his agitation, notwithstanding all his efforts. On learning the news the Czarina began to weep, and the Grand-Duchesses likewise dissolved into tears on seeing their mother's distress.[1]

At nine o'clock Sazonoff arrived at Alexandria. He was closeted with the Czar for a long time, and the latter also received Sir George Buchanan, the Ambassador of Great Britain, in the course of the evening.

I did not see the Czar again until after lunch the next day, when he came up to kiss the Czarevitch[2] before leaving for the solemn session at the WinterPalace, at which, in accordance with traditional usage, he was to issue a manifesto to his people announcing the war with Germany. He looked even worse than on the previous evening, and his eyes sparkled as if he had the fever. He told me he had just heard that the Germans had entered Luxemburg and attacked French customs houses before war was declared on France.

I will reproduce here some of the notes I made in my diary about this time.

Monday, August 3rd.—The Czar came up to Alexis Nicolaïevitch's room this morning. He was a changed

---

[1] I had these details from the Grand-Duchess Anastasie Nicolaïevna, who described the scene to me next morning.

[2] Alexis Nicolaïevitch had not recovered from his accident when he made his condition worse by an imprudent act. He was thus unable to accompany his parents to St. Petersburg—a great blow to them.

man. Yesterday's ceremony resolved itself into an impressive manifestation. When he appeared on the balcony of the Winter Palace the enormous crowd which had collected on the square fell on their knees and sang the Russian National Anthem. The enthusiasm of his · people has shown the Czar that this is unquestionably a national war.

I hear that at the Winter Palace yesterday the Czar took a solemn oath not to make peace while a single enemy soldier remains on Russian soil. In taking such an oath before the whole world Nicholas II. shows the true character of this war. It is a matter of life and death, a struggle for existence.

The Czarina had a long talk with me this afternoon. She was in a state of great indignation, as she had just heard that on orders from the Emperor William II. the Dowager-Empress of Russia had been prevented from continuing her journey to St. Petersburg and had had to go from Berlin to Copenhagen.

" Fancy a monarch arresting an Empress ! How could he descend to that ? He has absolutely changed since the militarist party, who hate Russia, have gained the upper hand with him. But I am sure he has been won over to the war against his will. He's been dragged into it by the Crown Prince, who openly assumed the leadership of the pan-German militarists and seemed to disapprove of his father's policy. He has forced his father's hand.

"I have never liked the Emperor William, if only because he is not sincere. He is vain and has always played the comedian. He was always reproaching me with doing nothing for Germany, and has always done his best to separate Russia and France,[1] though I never believed it was for the good of Russia. He will never forgive me this war !

" You know that the Czar received a telegram from him the night before last. It arrived several hours after the declaration of war, and demanded ' an immediate reply, which alone could avert the terrible disaster.' He thus tried to deceive the Czar once more, unless the telegram was kept back at Berlin by those who were bent on war in any case."

Tuesday, August 4th.—Germany has declared war on France and I hear that Switzerland also has mobilised, I have been to the Legation to get the orders for my ultimate departure.

Wednesday, August 5th.—I met the Czar in the park. He told me with immense pleasure that, as a result of the violation of the neutrality of Belgium, England has joined the great cause. The neutrality of Italy seems assured as well.

We have already won a great diplomatic victory. Military victory will follow, and, thanks to the help of England, it will come sooner than we think. The Germans have against them the whole of Europe, with the exception of Austria. Their insolence and despotism have at last been too much even for their allies. Look at the Italians !

This evening I had another long talk with the

---

[1] I cannot say that the Czarina had any personal affection for France, a country with which she had no ties and no particular temperamental affinity. She did not understand the French mind, and took all the literary acrobatics of our " *immoralistes* " quite seriously. On the other hand, she thoroughly enjoyed the great nineteenth-century poets.

Czarina, who will not hear of my leaving for Switzerland.

" It's ridiculous ! You will never get there. All communications are interrupted."

I told her that an arrangement had been made between the French Embassy and the Swiss Legation, and that we should all go home together *via* the Dardanelles.

" The trouble is that, if you have some chance—it's a very small one—of getting home, you will have *no* chance of getting back here before the end of the war. As Switzerland will not fight, you will be at home doing nothing."

At that moment Dr. Derevenko entered the room. In his hand he held an evening paper announcing the violation of Swiss neutrality by Germany.

" Again ! They must be crazy, mad ! " cried the Czarina. " They have absolutely lost their heads ! "

Realising she could not keep me now, she abandoned her resistance and began to speak kindly of my relations, who will be without news of me for some considerable time.

" I myself have no news of my brother," she added. " Where is he ? In Belgium or on the French front ? I shiver to think that the Emperor William may avenge himself against me by sending him to the Russian front. He is quite capable of such monstrous behaviour ! What a horrible war this is ! What evil and suffering it means ! . . . What will become of Germany ? What humiliation, what a downfall is in store for her ? And all for the sins of the Hohenzollerns—their idiotic pride and insatiable ambition. Whatever has happened to the

Germany of my childhood ? I have such happy and poetic memories of my early years in Darmstadt and the good friends I had there. But on my later visits Germany seemed to me a changed country—a country I did not know and had never known. . . . I had no community of thought or feeling with anyone except the old friends of days gone by. Prussia has meant Germany's ruin. The German people have been deceived. Feelings of hatred and revenge which are quite foreign to their nature have been instilled into them. It will be a terrible, monstrous struggle, and humanity is about to pass through ghastly sufferings. . . ."

Thursday, August 6th.—I went into the town this morning. The violation of the neutrality of Switzerland is not confirmed and seems most improbable. It is impossible to travel *via* the Dardanelles. Our departure is thus postponed, and we cannot say when it will take place. This uncertainty makes me anxious.

Sunday, August 9th.—The Czar has had another long talk with me to-day. As before, he expressed himself with a confidence and frankness which can only be explained by the exceptional circumstances through which we are passing. Neither he nor the Czarina ever used to discuss political or personal questions with me. But the amazing events of the last few days, and the fact that I have been so intimately associated with their troubles and anxieties, have drawn me closer to them, and for the time being the conventional barriers of etiquette and Court usage have fallen.

The Czar first spoke to me about the solemn session of the Duma on the previous day. He told me how

THE CZAR AND THE CZAREVITCH EXAMINING THE FIRST MACHINE-GUN CAPTURED FROM THE GERMANS. PETERHOF, AUGUST, 1914.

THE CZAR AND THE CZAREVITCH BEFORE THE PARBED WIRE.
WHITE RUSSIA, AUTUMN, 1915.

[Facing page 110.

tremendously pleased he had been with its resolute and dignified attitude and its fervent patriotism.

" The Duma was in every way worthy of the occasion. It expressed the real will of the nation, for the whole of Russia smarts under the insults heaped upon it by Germany. I have the greatest confidence in the future now. . . . Speaking personally, I have done everything in my power to avert this war, and I am ready to make any concessions consistent with our dignity and national honour. You cannot imagine how glad I am that all the uncertainty is over, for I have never been through so terrible a time as the days preceding the outbreak of war. I am sure that there will now be a national uprising in Russia like that of the great war of 1812."

Wednesday, August 12th.—It is Alexis Nicolaïe-vitch's birthday. He is ten to-day.

Friday, August 14th.—The Grand-Duke Nicholas Nicolaïevitch,[1] Commander-in-Chief of the Russian Armies, has left for the front. Before leaving Peterhof he came to Alexandria to give the Czar the first trophy of the war, a machine-gun captured from the Germans in one of the skirmishes which have marked the commencement of operations on the East Prussian frontier.

Saturday, August 15th.—I was told last night that my return to Switzerland has been officially excused. I am told this is the result of the action M. Sazonoff has taken at Berne at Her Majesty's suggestion. In any

---

[1] He was the grandson of the Czar Nicholas I., and had been appointed Generalissimo of the Russian armies immediately after the declaration of war.

case, it is more and more doubtful whether the Swiss will be able to get away.

The Imperial family is to go on the 17th to Moscow where the Czar will observe the traditional custom and ask the blessing of God on himself and his people in the tragic hours through which the country is passing.

Monday, August 17th.—The arrival of Their Majesties at Moscow has been one of the most impressive and moving sights I have ever seen in my life.

After the customary reception at the station we went in a long file of carriages towards the Kremlin. An enormous crowd had collected in the squares and in the streets, climbed on the roofs of the shops, into the branches of trees. They swarmed in the shop windows and filled the balconies and windows of the houses. While all the bells of the churches were ringing as if they would never stop, from those thousands of throats poured that wonderful Russian National Anthem, so overwhelming with its religious grandeur and pent emotion, in which the faith of a whole race is embodied :

> " God save the Czar !
> Mighty and powerful, let him reign for our glory,
> For the confusion of our enemies, the orthodox Czar.
> God save the Czar ! "

On the steps of the churches, through the great doorways of which one could see the light of the candles burning before the reliquaries, the priests in vestments, and holding their great crucifixes in both hands, blessed the Czar as he passed. The hymn stopped, and then began again, rising like a prayer with a mighty and majestic rhythm :

> " God save the Czar ! "

The procession arrived at the Iberian Gate.[1] The Czar got out of his carriage and, in accordance with custom, entered the chapel to kiss the miraculous image of the Virgin of Iberia. He came out, walked a little way, and then stopped, high above the immense multitude. His face was grave and composed. He stood motionless to hear the voice of his people. He seemed to be in silent communion with them. Once again he could hear the great heart of Russia beating. . . .

He then turned again towards the chapel, crossed himself, put on his cap, and slowly walked to his carriage, which disappeared under the old gate and went towards the Kremlin.

Alexis Nicolaïevitch is complaining a good deal of his leg again to-night. Will he be able to walk to-morrow or will he have to be carried when Their Majesties go to the Cathedral ? The Czar and Czarina are in despair. The boy was not able to be present at the ceremony in the Winter Palace. It is always the same when he is supposed to appear in public. You can be practically certain that some complication will prevent it. Fate seems to pursue him.

Tuesday, August 18*th.*—When Alexis Nicolaïevitch found he could not walk this morning he was in a terrible state. Their Majesties have decided that he shall be present at the ceremony all the same. He will be carried by one of the Czar's cossacks. But it is a dreadful disappointment to the parents, who do not

---

[1] This is the gate by which the Czars always entered to go to the Kremlin when they visited Moscow. It leads from the city to the Red Square, which is against the eastern wall of the Kremlin.

wish the idea to gain ground among the people that the Heir to the Throne is an invalid.

At eleven o'clock, when the Czar appeared at the top of the Red Staircase, the huge crowd in the square gave him a magnificent reception. He came down slowly, with the Czarina on his arm, and at the head of a long procession slowly crossed the bridge connecting the palace with the Cathedral of the Assumption and entered the church amid a frantic outburst of cheering from the crowd. The Metropolitan Bishops of Kiev, St. Petersburg, and Moscow and the high dignitaries of the Orthodox clergy were present. When Mass was over, the members of the Imperial family in turn approached the holy relics and kissed them. Then they knelt at the tombs of the patriarchs. Afterwards they went to the Monastery of Miracles to pray at the tomb of St. Alexis.

Long after Their Majesties had returned to the palace the crowd continued to collect in the square in the hope of seeing them again. Even when we came out several hours later there were still hundreds of peasants outside the palace.

Thursday, August 20th.—Popular enthusiasm is waxing from day to day. It seems as if the people of Moscow are so proud of having their Czar with them, and so anxious to keep him as long as possible, that they mean to hold him here by manifest proofs of their affection. The manifestations are increasingly spontaneous, enthusiastic, and expressive.

Alexis and I drive out in a car every morning. As a rule we go to the Monks' Hill, from which there is a magnificent view of the valley of the Moskova and the city of the Czars. It was from this spot that Napoleon gazed on Moscow before entering it on September 14th, 1812. It is certainly a marvellous view. In the foreground, at the foot of the hill, is the Monastery of Novo-Dievitchy, with its fortified *enceinte* and sixteen castellated towers. A little further back is the Holy City, with its four hundred and fifty churches, its palaces and parks, its monasteries with their crenellated walls, its gilded cupolas and innumerable domes of brilliant colours and strange shapes.

As we were coming back from our usual drive this morning, so dense was the crowd that the chauffeur was obliged to stop in one of the rather narrow streets in the Yakimanskaïa quarter. The crowd consisted of humble folk and peasants from the district who had come into the city to shop or in the hope of seeing the Czar. All at once there was a loud shout : " The Heir ! . . . The Heir ! . . ." The crowd surged towards us, surrounded us, and came up so close that our way was blocked, and we, so to speak, found ourselves prisoners of these *moujiks*, workmen and shopkeepers who struggled and fought, shouted, gesticulated, and behaved like lunatics in order to get a better view of the Czarevitch. By degrees some of the women and children grew bolder, mounted the steps of the car, thrust their arms over the doors, and when they succeeded in touching the boy they yelled out triumphantly : " I've touched him ! . . . I've touched the Heir ! . . ."

Alexis Nicolaïevitch, frightened at these exuberant demonstrations, was sitting far back in the car. He was very pale, startled by this sudden popular manifestation, which was taking extravagant forms which were quite novel to him. He recovered himself, however, when he saw the kindly smiles of the crowd, but he remained embarrassed at the attention bestowed upon him, not knowing what to say or do.

Personally, I was speculating, not without considerable anxiety, how all this would end, for I knew that no police regulations are issued for the Czarevitch's drives as neither the time nor the route can be fixed beforehand. I began to fear that we might meet with some accident in the middle of this unruly crowd swarming round us.

To my relief two huge *gorodovy* (policemen) came up, puffing and blowing, shouting and storming. The crowd displayed the unquestioning and resigned obedience of the *moujik*. It began to waver, then slowly drifted away. I then told Derevenko, who was following in another car, to go ahead, and by degrees we succeeded in getting clear.

Friday, August 21st.—Their Majesties, before returning to Tsarskoïe-Selo, decided to visit the Troïtsa Monastery, the most celebrated sanctuary in Russia after the world-famed *Laure* of Kiev. The train took us as far as the little station of Serghievo, from which we reached the monastery by car. Perched on a hill, it would be taken for a fortified city from a distance if the bright-coloured towers and gilded domes of its thirteen churches did not betray its true purpose. In the course of its history this rampart of Orthodoxy has had to resist some formidable assaults, the most famous being the sixteen months' siege by an army of thirty thousand Poles at the beginning of the seventeenth century.

This monastery, like Moscow and the towns of the Upper Volga, is a spot where the past seems ever present. It calls up visions of the Russia of the boyarin, the Grand-Dukes of Moscow, and the first Czars, and vividly explains the historical evolution of the Russian people.

The Imperial family were present at a *Te Deum* and knelt before the relics of St. Sergius, the founder of the monastery. The Archimandrite then handed the Czar an icon painted in a fragment of the coffin of the saint, one of the most revered in Russia. In olden times this image always accompanied the Czars on their campaigns. On the Czar's orders it is being sent to General Head-quarters and placed in the " field chapel " of the Commander-in-Chief of the Russian Armies.

The Czar, Czarina, and their children visited the little church of Saint Nicon and then stayed a few minutes in the ancient residence of the patriarchs. As time was pressing, we had to abandon the idea of visiting the hermitage of Gethsemane, which is a little distance from the monastery. In accordance with a practice still frequently observed in Russia, certain hermits still have themselves shut up here in subterranean walled cells. They live in prayer and fasting to the end of their days, completely isolated from the world, and the slit through which their food is passed is their sole means of communication with their fellow-men.

The Imperial family bade the Archimandrite farewell and left the monastery, accompanied by a crowd of monks who swarmed round the cars.

CHAPTER X
THE FIRST SIX MONTHS OF THE WAR

CHAPTER X

THE FIRST SIX MONTHS OF THE WAR

ON August 22nd we returned to Tsarskoïe-Selo, where the Czar was to be obliged to spend some time before he could get away to General Headquarters. Decisions of the utmost importance required his presence near the capital.

Notwithstanding the terrible weight of responsibility on his shoulders, the Czar never showed such firmness, resolution, and conscious energy as during this period at the beginning of the war. His personal influence had never been exerted with more authority. It seemed as if he had devoted himself body and soul to the formidable task of leading Russia to victory. We felt he was inspired by some inward force and a dour determination to conquer which communicated itself to everyone with whom he came in contact.

The Czar was shy and retiring by nature. He belonged to the category of human beings who are always hesitating because they are too diffident and are ever slow to impose their will on others because they are too gentle and sensitive. He had little faith in himself and imagined that he was one of the unlucky ones. Unfortunately his life seemed to show that he was not entirely wrong. Hence his doubts and hesitations. But this time it seemed as if he had changed. What was it gave him his confidence?

In the first place the Czar believed that his cause was a

holy cause.   The events of the end of July had enabled him to
see through the duplicity of Germany to which he had nearly
fallen a victim.   He also felt that he had never been so near
to his people.   He seemed to be borne along by them.   His
journey to Moscow had shown him how popular the war was
and how much the nation appreciated the fact that his firm and
dignified attitude had enhanced its prestige in the eyes of the
outside world.   The enthusiasm of the masses had never before
been demonstrated with the same spontaneous fervour.   He
felt that he had the whole country behind him, and he hoped
that political passion, which had vanished in the presence of
the common peril, would not revive so long as the war was in
progress.

The disaster of Soldau, in East Prussia, occurred a few days
after his arrival in Moscow, but it had not shaken his confidence.
He knew the cause of that terrible defeat had been that
the concentration of the troops had not been complete, and
that General Samsonoff's army had had to advance into German
territory too fast in order to attract some of the enemy forces
to itself and thus relieve the Western Front.   That defeat had
had its compensation a week later in the victory of the Marne.
It was not right to bewail a sacrifice which had saved France
and therefore ultimately Russia herself.   It is true that the
same result could have been obtained with less loss and that
the Russian High Command was not free from blame, but this
was one of the misfortunes which are always possible in the
early days of a campaign.

The Czar thus preserved all his confidence and energy.   At
the very beginning of the war, and notwithstanding the
opposition of many influential people, he had prohibited the
production and sale of spirits.   The step meant a serious loss

to the Treasury, and that at a time when money was wanted more than ever. But his faith had been stronger than all the objections which had been urged. He had also acted personally ⁊. in endeavouring to replace all unpopular Ministers by men who seemed to have the confidence of the Duma. In that way he desired to emphasise his wish for closer collaboration with the representatives of the people.

On October 3rd the Czar had gone to G.H.Q., where he spent three days. Then after a short visit to the troops in the region of Brest and Kovno, he had returned to Tsarskoïe-Selo.

Henceforth he made periodic visits to the front and the interior of the country, seeing the different sectors of the immense front, the clearing stations and military hospitals, the factories and, in fact, everything which played any part in the conduct of the terrible war.

The Czarina had devoted herself to the cause of the wounded from the start, and she had decided that the Grand-Duchesses Olga Nicolaïevna and Tatiana Nicolaïevna should assist her in her task. All three of them took a course in nursing, and passed several hours of every day caring for the wounded who were sent to Tsarskoïe-Selo. Her Majesty, sometimes with the Czar and sometimes alone with her two daughters, paid several visits to the Red Cross establishments in the towns of Western and Central Russia. At her suggestion, many military hospitals had been organised, as well as ambulance trains specially fitted up for the evacuation of the wounded to the rear, a process which was often very slow owing to the immense distances. Her example had been followed, and private initiative had never been displayed with the same enthusiasm and generosity.

Lastly a congress of all the *zemstvos* [1] and the municipalities of Russia had assembled in Moscow to organise the resources of the country. Under the influence of energetic and disinterested individuals the congress had rapidly been converted into a potent piece of machinery, with immense resources at its command and in a position to give the Government the most valuable help.

In its scope and the patriotic fervour behind it this movement had been unprecedented in Russian history. The war had become a truly national war.

The month of September had been marked for Russia by alternating victories and reverses. In East Prussia the defeat of Tannenberg had been followed by that of the Masurian Lakes, where the superiority of the Germans had been demonstrated once again. In Galicia, on the other hand, the Russians had captured Lemberg, and continued their irresistible advance, inflicting serious losses on the Austrian army, which had fallen back into the Carpathians. In the following month the Germans tried to secure Warsaw, but their furious onslaught had been broken against the splendid resistance of the Russians. The losses on both sides had been heavy.

In December the Czar paid a visit to the Caucasus, where the Southern Army was operating. He was anxious to spend a little time with the troops who were fighting under the most trying conditions against the Turkish divisions massed on the Armenian frontier. On his return he joined the Czarina at Moscow, and the children also were brought there to meet him. The Czar visited the military schools and with Her

---

[1] In the 39 Governments of Russia the executive authorities were assisted by the provincial assemblies (*zemstvos*), who looked after the economic interests of the Government, the establishment of schools, hospitals, etc. There were also district *zemstvos* in the same Governments.

Majesty, his son and daughters, several times made the rounds
of the hospitals and nursing establishments in that city. ₁ₐₗₗ ·

During the five days we spent at Moscow the enthusiasm
of the people had been every bit as great as in August, and it
was with real regret that Their Majesties left the ancient capital
of Muscovy, the Czar leaving for G.H.Q. and the other members
of the family returning to Tsarskoïe-Selo.

After the New Year's Day celebrations the Czar resumed
his periodical visits to the front. The army was then preparing
for the great offensive which was to take place in March.

Throughout this winter the health of the Czarevitch had
been very satisfactory, and his lessons could proceed along
regular lines. In the early spring Her Majesty informed me
that the Czar and she had decided, in view of the circumstances, to dispense with the appointment of a *vospitatiet* for
Alexis Nicolaïevitch for the moment. Contrary to my ex-
pectations, I thus found myself compelled to shoulder the
immense burden of responsibility alone for some time longer,
and to find some means of filling up the gaps in the Heir's
education. I had a strong feeling that it was essential that
he should get away from his ordinary environment, even if it
were only for a few hours a day, and try to establish contact
with real life. I applied for and obtained a General Staff map
of the country, and I planned a series of motor drives which
enabled us gradually to cover all the district around within a
radius of twenty miles. We used to start out immediately
after lunch, and often stopped at villages to watch the peasants
at work. Alexis Nicolaïevitch liked questioning them, and
they always answered him with the frank, kindly simplicity of
the Russian *moujik*, not having the slightest idea whom they

were speaking to. The railway lines of the suburbs of St. Petersburg had a great attraction for the boy. He took the liveliest interest in the activities of the little stations we passed and the work of repair on the track, bridges, etc.

The palace police grew alarmed at these excursions, which took us beyond the guarded zone, especially as our route was not known beforehand. I was asked to observe the rules in force, but I disregarded them, and our drives continued as before. The police then changed their procedure, and whenever we left the park we were certain to see a car appear and follow in our tracks. It was one of Alexis Nicolaïevitch's greatest delights to try and throw it off the scent, and now and then we were successful.

My particular anxiety, however, was to find companions for the Imperial Heir. This was a problem most difficult to solve. Fortunately circumstances themselves conspired to make good this deficiency to a certain extent. Dr. Derevenko had a son who was almost the same age as Alexis Nicolaïevitch. The two boys got to know each other, and were soon good friends. No Sunday, *fête* day or holiday passed without them meeting. They were together every day ultimately, and the Czarevitch even obtained permission to visit the house of Dr. Derevenko, who lived in a little villa not far from the palace. He often spent whole afternoons there with his friend and playmate in the modest home of a *bourgeois* family. There was a good deal of criticism of this innovation, but Their Majesties would not interfere. They were so unaffected in their own private life that they could not but encourage the same tastes in their children.

Yet the war had already brought some very remarkable change in our life at the palace. It had always been austere, and now became even more so. The Czar was away a good deal. The Czarina and her two elder daughters almost always wore the costume of a nurse, and divided their time between visits to the hospitals and the innumerable duties arising out of their work for the relief of the wounded. The Czarina was very tired even when the war began. She had spent herself without counting the consequences, devoting herself with the enthusiasm and ardour she brought to everything to which she set her hand. Although her health was severely shaken, she displayed remarkable physical elasticity. She seemed to derive comfort and strength from the accomplishment of the splendid task which she had undertaken. It was as if she found that it satisfied her craving for self-devotion and enabled her to forget the poignant anxiety and apprehension that the Czarevitch's illness caused, even in its inactive periods.

Another result of the war, as agreeable as unexpected, was that Rasputin had retired into the background. At the end of September he had returned from Siberia completely recovered from the terrible wound which had all but ended his days. But everything pointed to the fact that since his return he was being more or less neglected. In any case, his visits were more and more infrequent. It was true that as Alexis Nicolaï-evitch had been so much better during the winter there had been no need to resort to his intervention, so that he had found himself deprived of what had been his great stand-by.

But when all is said, his power remained quite formidable. I had proof of the fact a short time after, when Madame Wyroubova was all but killed in a terrible railway accident. She was nearly dead when she was dragged from under the fragments of a shattered carriage, and had been brought to Tsarskoïe-Selo in a condition which seemed desperate. In her terror the Czarina had rushed to the bedside of the woman who was almost her only friend. Rasputin, who had been hastily sent for, was there also.   In this accident the Czarina saw a new proof of the evil fate which seemed to pursue so relentlessly all those whom she loved.   As she asked Rasputin in a tone of anguish whether Madame Wyroubova would live, he replied :

" God will give her back to you if she is needed by you and the country.   If her influence is harmful, on the other hand, He will take her away.   I cannot claim to know His impenetrable designs."

It must be admitted that this was a very clever way of evading an awkward question. If Madame Wyroubova recovered he would have earned her eternal gratitude, as, thanks to him, her recovery would seem to consecrate, as it were, her mission with the Czarina.   If she died, on the other hand, Her Majesty would see in her death a manifestation of the inscrutable ways of Providence, and thus be the more easily consoled in her loss.[1]

Rasputin's intervention had helped him to recover his influence, but his triumph was short-lived.   In spite of everything, we felt that something had changed, and that he was not so important as he had been.   I was delighted to note the fact, particularly as shortly before I had had a long talk on the subject of the *staretz* with the Swiss Minister in Petrograd.[2] The information he gave me in the course of our conversation left me in no doubt as to the real character of Rasputin.   As I had always suspected, he was a misguided mystic who possessed a kind of psychic power, an unbalanced creature who

---

[1] Madame Wyroubova survived her injuries, but her convalescence was a very long and dreary process and she was always a cripple after her accident.

[2] By a ukase of August 31st, 1914, the Czar had decreed that St. Petersburg should henceforth be called Petrograd.

worked alternately through his carnal desires and his mystic' visions, a being quite capable of having weeks of religious ecstasy after nights of infamy. But before this interview I had never realised the importance that was attached to Rasputin's influence on politics, not merely in Russian circles, but even in the embassies and legations of Petrograd. That influence was greatly exaggerated, but the mere fact that it could exist was a kind of challenge to public opinion. The presence of this man at Court was also a subject of mystery and abhorrence to all who knew the debauchery of his private life. I fully realised that all this involved the greatest danger to the prestige of Their Majesties and furnished a weapon which their enemies would sooner or later try to use against them.

The mischief could only have been remedied by sending Rasputin away ; but where was the power strong enough to bring about his disgrace ? I knew the deep, underlying causes of his hold over the Czarina too well not to fear the restoration of his influence if circumstances took a turn favourable to him.

The first six months of the war had not brought the results hoped for, and everything pointed to a long and bitter struggle. Unexpected complications might arise, for the prolongation of the war might well bring very serious economic difficulties which could foster general discontent and provoke actual disorder. The Czar and Czarina were much concerned at this aspect of the matter. It made them very anxious.

As ever in moments of trouble and uncertainty, it was from religion and the affection of their children that they drew the comfort they needed. With their usual natural simplicity and good humour the Grand-Duchesses had accepted the increasing austerity of life at Court. It is true that their own

I

lives, so utterly destitute of the elements which young girls find most agreeable, had prepared them for the change. When war broke out in 1914, Olga Nicolaïevna was nineteen and Tatiana Nicolaïevna had just had her seventeenth birthday. They had never been to a ball. The only parties at which they had appeared were one or two given by their aunt, the Grand-Duchess Olga Alexandrovna. After hostilities one thought, and one thought alone, inspired them—to relieve the cares and anxieties of their parents by surrounding them with a love which revealed itself in the most touching and delicate attentions.

If only the world had known what an example the Imperial family were setting with their tender and intimate association ! But how few ever suspected it ! For it was too indifferent to public opinion and avoided the public gaze.

CHAPTER XI

THE RETREAT OF THE RUSSIAN ARMY—
THE CZAR PLACES HIMSELF AT THE HEAD
OF HIS ARMY—THE GROWING INFLUENCE
OF THE CZARINA
(FEBRUARY—SEPTEMBER, 1915)

CHAPTER XI

THE RETREAT OF THE RUSSIAN ARMY— THE CZAR PLACES HIMSELF AT THE HEAD OF HIS ARMY—THE GROWING INFLUENCE OF THE CZARINA (FEBRUARY—SEPTEMBER, 1915)

IN spite of the successes gained by the Russians in Galicia in the autumn, the situation was very uncertain in the spring of 1915. On both sides preparations were being made for a fierce renewal of the struggle to which the fighting of January and February was only the prelude. On the Russian side it looked as if everything possible had been done to strengthen the army's fighting power and assure the normal flow of supplies. The Czar, at any rate, believed that it was so, on the faith of the reports he had received. He had placed all his hopes on the success of this spring campaign.

The Austrians were the first to take the offensive, but the Russians counter-attacked vigorously, and their superiority was soon made manifest all along the front. In the first fortnight of March their successes were continued. On the 19th they captured the fortress of Przemysl. The whole garrison and considerable booty in war material fell into their hands. There was tremendous excitement in the country. The Czar returned from G.H.Q. on March 24th. He was in high spirits.   Were the fortunes of war at length going to turn in favour of Russia ?

In the middle of April Russian divisions stood on the crest of the Carpathians and menaced the rich plains of Hungary. The Austrian army was at the end of its tether.   But these successes had been bought at the price of enormous losses, and the mountain fighting continued under conditions which were extremely trying even for the victor.   The prolongation of the war was also beginning to show effects on the population at home.   It had begun to feel the high cost of food and the poverty of communications was paralysing all economic life. There must be no delay in finding a solution.

But Germany could not remain indifferent to the dissolution of the Austrian army, and as soon as she clearly appreciated the danger she made up her mind to avert it by taking every step in her power.   Several German army corps had been massed east of Cracow and placed under the command of General Mackensen, who was to take the offensive against the flank of the Russian army and try to cut the communications of the troops operating in the Carpathians.   The onslaught began in the first days of May, and under the pressure of the Germans the Russian army of Western Galicia was obliged to retreat rapidly to the east.   It had to accept the loss of the Carpathians, the capture of which had cost so much blood and effort, and descend into the plains.   The troops fought with remarkable courage and endurance, but they were cruelly short of arms and ammunition.

The retreat continued.   On June 5th Przemysl was lost, and on June 22nd Lemberg.   By the end of the month all Galicia—that Slav land the conquest of which had filled all Russian hearts with joy—had been evacuated.

THE CZAR.

THE CZAREVITCH.

[Facing page 134.

Meanwhile the Germans had begun a vigorous offensive in Poland and made rapid progress in spite of the fierce resistance of the Russians.   It was a grave moment.   The whole Russian front had been shaken and given way under the pressure of the Austro-German armies.   Men wished to know who was responsible for these disasters.   They called for the guilty and demanded their punishment.

The development of events had been a terrible blow to the Czar.   It had been a shock, especially as he had certainly not expected anything of the kind.   But he set his teeth against adversity.   On June 25th he dismissed the Minister of War, General Sukhomlinoff, whose criminal negligence seemed to have been responsible for the fact that it was impossible to secure the army's supplies.   He replaced him by General Polivanoff.   On the 27th he summoned a conference at G.H.Q., at which all the Ministers were present.   It was a question of rousing all the energies of the country, of mobilising all its forces and resources for the life-and-death struggle with the hated foe.

It was decided to summon the Duma.   The first sitting took place on August 1st, the anniversary of the declaration of war by Germany on Russia.   The firm and courageous attitude of the Assembly did a good deal to calm the public agitation. But while calling on the whole nation to co-operate in the defence of the Fatherland, the Duma demanded that the guilty should be discovered and punished.   A few days later the Czar appointed a " Commission of Enquiry " with a view to fixing responsibility for the nation's misfortunes.

Meanwhile the German offensive in Poland had made further progress.   On August 5th Warsaw was abandoned by the Russians, who withdrew to the right bank of the Vistula.

On the 17th Kovno was lost. One after the other all the Russian fortresses fell before the onslaught of the enemy, whose advance no obstacle seemed capable of staying. By the end of August the whole of the Government of Poland was in the hands of the Germans.

The reverses assumed the proportions of a catastrophe which endangered the very existence of the country. Should we be able to stop the invading hordes or should we have to follow the precedent of 1812 and withdraw into the interior, thus abandoning Russian soil to the enemy? Had all our willing sacrifices brought us nothing?

The country was suffering from the incessant withdrawals of men and from requisitions. Agriculture was short of labour and horses. In the towns the cost of living was rising with the disorganisation of the railways and the influx of refugees. The most pessimistic news passed from mouth to mouth. There was talk of sabotage, treason, etc. Russian public opinion, so changeable and prone to exaggeration whether in joy or sorrow, indulged in the most gloomy forebodings.

It was just when Russia was passing through this acute crisis that Nicholas II. decided to take the command of his armies in person.

For several months the Czarina had been urging the Czar to take this step, but he had stood out against her suggestion as he did not like the idea of relieving the Grand-Duke Nicholas of the post he had given him. When the war broke out his first impulse had been to put himself at the head of his army, but, yielding to the representations of his Ministers, he had abandoned an idea which was very close to his heart. He had always regretted it, and now that the Germans had conquered all Poland and were advancing on Russian soil, he considered it nothing less than criminal to remain away from the front and not take a more active part in the defence of his country.

The Czar had returned from G.H.Q. on July 11th, and spent two months at Tsarskoïe-Selo before making up his mind to this new step. I will relate a conversation I had with him on July 16th, as it shows quite clearly what were the ideas that inspired him at that time. On that day he had joined Alexis Nicolaïevitch and myself in the park, and had just been telling his son something about his recent visit to the army. Turning to me, he added :

" You have no idea how depressing it is to be away from the front. It seems as if everything here saps energy and enfeebles resolution. The most pessimistic rumours and the most ridiculous stories are accepted and get about everywhere. Folk here care nothing except for intrigues and cabals, and regard low personal interests only. Out at the front men fight and die for their country. At the front there is only one thought—the determination to conquer. All else is forgotten, and, in spite of our losses and our reverses, everyone remains confident. Any man fit to bear arms should be in the army. Speaking for myself, I can never be in too much of a hurry to be with my troops." [1]

The Czarina was able to take advantage of this great ambition. She set herself to overcome the scruples which considerations of another character inspired. She desired the removal of the Grand-Duke Nicholas, whom she accused of secretly working for the ruin of the Czar's reputation and prestige and for a palace revolution which would further his

---

[1] It was the same sentiment which made him say to an officer of his suite after his abdication : " Just to think that, now I am Czar no longer, they won't even let me fight for my country ! " The words reveal the very depths of his soul.

own ends.   On the strength of certain information she had received from Madame Wyroubova, she was also persuaded that G.H.Q. was the centre of a plot, the object of which was to seize her during the absence of her husband and confine her in a convent.

The Czar, on the other hand, had full confidence in the loyalty of the Grand-Duke Nicholas. He considered him incapable of any criminal action, but he was compelled to admit his complicity in the intrigue against the Czarina.   Yet he did not give way until the imperious instinct urging him to put himself at the head of his army had become an obligation of conscience.   By intervening personally in the struggle he hoped to show the world that the war would be fought out to the bitter end and prove his own unshakable faith in ultimate victory.   In this tragic hour he thought it was his duty to stake his own person, and as head of the state to assume the full burden of responsibility.   By his presence among the troops he wished to restore their confidence, for their *morale* had been shaken by the long series of reverses, and they were tired of fighting against an enemy whose strength consisted principally in the superiority of his armament.

In spite of the recent retreats, the prestige of the Grand-Duke Nicholas was still considerable in Russia.   During this first twelve months of the war he had given proof of resolution and an iron will.   The fact that he was deprived of his command in times of defeat indicated that he was held responsible, and was bound to be interpreted as a punishment, as unjust on the merits as insulting to his honour.   The Czar fully realised all this, and only decided as he did much against his will.   His first idea had been to keep the Grand-Duke with him at G.H.Q., but that would have made the position of the ex-Generalissimo somewhat delicate. The Czar decided to appoint him Lieutenant-General of the Caucasus and Commander-in-Chief of the army operating against the Turks.

The Czar communicated his decision to take over the Supreme Command to his Ministers at a council which took place at Tsarskoïe-Selo a few days before his departure for G.H.Q. The news threw most of those present into utter consternation, and they did their best to dissuade him from his project. They pointed to the grave difficulties in the way of public business if the head of the state was to spend practically all his time at G.H.Q., more than five hundred miles from the seat of government. They referred to his innumerable duties and asked him not to take new and crushing responsibilities upon himself. In the last resort they begged him not to place himself at the head of his troops at a moment so critical. In case of failure he was running a risk of exposing himself to attacks which would undermine his prestige and authority.

Yet the Czar was not to be moved. Several members of his immediate *entourage* made several further attempts to convince him, but these failed also, and on the evening of September 4th he left for Mohileff, where G.H.Q. was established at that time. The next day he signed the *Prikase*, in which he announced to the troops that he was taking command in person, and at the foot he added in his own hand :

"With unshakable faith in the goodness of God and firm confidence in final victory we shall accomplish our sacred duty in defending our Fatherland to the end, and we shall never let the soil of Russia be outraged."

He was repeating the oath he had taken at the outset of the war and casting his crown into the arena.

In France and England this announcement came as a

surprise which was not without a certain element of apprehension, but this action was regarded as a pledge which irrevocably associated the Russian Empire, in the person of its Czar, with the fortunes of the Entente, and this at a moment when a series of defeats would have been grounds for fearing separatist tendencies. All the great newspapers of the Allied countries emphasised the importance of this decision. It was hoped that it would have a considerable effect on the *morale* of the Russian army and contribute to further the cause of final victory. In Russia the whole Press raised a shout of triumph, but in sober reality opinion about the wisdom of changing the command was sharply divided at first. In the army itself we shall see that the presence of the Czar helped to raise the spirits and courage of the men and gave the campaign a new impetus.

History will some day reveal the political and military consequences of this step, which was certainly an act of courage and faith on the part of the Czar himself.

As I had feared, the apparent indifference with which Rasputin had been treated during the winter had only been temporary, and at the time of the disasters in May there was a revival of his influence, which grew steadily stronger. The change is easily explained. At the beginning of the war the Czar and Czarina were utterly obsessed by the greatness of their task, and had passed through hours of exaltation in the knowledge of the love they bore their people, a love they felt was reciprocated. That fervent communion had filled them with hope. They believed that they were really the centre of that great national movement which swept over the whole of Russia. The military events of the following months had not shaken their courage. They had maintained their ardent faith

THE CZARINA.

THE FOUR GRAND-DUCHESSES.

[*Facing page* 140.

in that spring offensive which was to bring about the final success of the Russian armies.

When the great catastrophe followed they passed through a time of unspeakable anguish. In her sorrow the Czarina was bound to feel impelled to seek moral support from him whom she already regarded not only as the saviour of her son, but as the representative of the people, sent by God to save Russia and her husband also.

It is not true that personal ambition or a thirst for power induced the Czarina to intervene in political affairs. Her motive was purely sentimental. She worshipped her husband as she worshipped her children, and there was no limit to her devotion for those she loved. Her only desire was to be useful to the Czar in his heavy task and to help him with her counsel.

Convinced that autocracy was the only form of government suited to the needs of Russia, the Czarina believed that any great concessions to liberal demands were premature. In her view the uneducated masses of the Russian people could be galvanised into action only by a Czar in whose person all power was centralised. She was certain that to the *moujik* the Czar was the symbol of the unity, greatness, and glory of Russia, the head of the state and the Lord's Anointed. To encroach on his prerogatives was to undermine the faith of the Russian peasant and to risk precipitating the worst disasters for the country. The Czar must not merely rule : he must govern the state with a firm and mighty hand.

To the new task the Czarina brought the same devotion, courage, and, alas ! blindness she had shown in her fight for the life of her son. She was at any rate logical in her errors. Persuaded, as she was, that the only support for the dynasty was the nation, and that Rasputin was God's elect (had she not witnessed the efficacy of his prayers during her son's illness ?), she was absolutely convinced that this lowly peasant could use his supernatural powers to help him who held in his hands the fate of the empire of the Czars.

Cunning and astute as he was, Rasputin never advised in political matters except with the most extreme caution. He always took the greatest care to be very well informed as to what was going on at Court and as to the private feelings of the Czar and his wife. As a rule, therefore, his prophecies only confirmed the secret wishes of the Czarina. In fact, it was almost impossible to doubt that it was she who inspired the " inspired," but as her desires were interpreted by Rasputin, they seemed in her eyes to have the sanction and authority of a revelation.

Before the war the influence of the Czarina in political affairs had been but intermittent. It was usually confined to procuring the dismissal of anyone who declared his hostility to the *staretz*. In the first months of the war there had been no change in that respect, but after the great reverses in the spring of 1915, and more particularly after the Czar had assumed command of the army, the Czarina played an ever-increasing part in affairs of state because she wished to help her husband, who was overwhelmed with the burden of his growing responsibilities. She was worn out, and desired nothing more than peace and rest, but she willingly sacrificed her personal comfort to what she believed was a sacred duty.

Very reserved and yet very impulsive, the Czarina, first and foremost the wife and mother, was never happy except in the bosom of her family. She was artistic and well-educated, and liked reading and the arts. She was fond of meditation, and often became wholly absorbed in her own inward thoughts and feelings, an absorption from which she would only emerge when danger threatened. She would throw herself at the obstacle with all the ardour of a passionate nature. She was endowed with the finest moral qualities, and was always inspired by the highest ideals. But her sorrows had broken her. She was but the shadow of her former self, and she often had periods of mystic ecstasy in which she lost all sense of reality. Her faith in Rasputin proves it beyond a doubt.

It was thus that in her desire to save her husband and son, whom she loved more than life itself, she forged with her own hands the instrument of their undoing.

CHAPTER XII

NICHOLAS II. AS COMMANDER-IN-CHIEF—THE ARRIVAL OF THE CZAREVITCH AT G.H.Q.— VISITS TO THE FRONT (SEPTEMBER—DECEMBER, 1915)

CHAPTER XII

NICHOLAS II. AS COMMANDER-IN-CHIEF—THE ARRIVAL OF THE CZAREVITCH AT G.H.Q.— VISITS TO THE FRONT (SEPTEMBER—DECEMBER, 1915)

THE Grand-Duke Nicholas left G.H.Q. on September 7th, two days after the arrival of the Czar. He left for the Caucasus, taking with him General Yanushkevitch, who had been replaced as First Quartermaster-General of the Russian armies by General Alexeieff a short time before. This appointment had been very well received by military circles, who had high hopes of Alexeieff. He it was who had drawn up the plan of campaign in Galicia in the autumn of 1914, and as Commander of the North-Western Front he had just given further proof of his military talent. The burden which was now laid upon his shoulders was a crushing one, for as a result of the irresistible advance of the Germans the Russian army was in a very critical position, and the decisions which he had to take were exceptionally grave. From the outset the Czar gave him an entirely free hand with regard to the operations, confining himself to covering him with his authority and taking responsibility for everything he did.

A few days after Nicholas II. took over the Supreme Command the situation suddenly took a turn for the worse. The Germans, who had massed large forces north-west of Vilnam, had succeeded in breaking the Russian front, and their cavalry was operating in the rear of the army and threatening its communications.   On September 18th we seemed on the verge of a great disaster.

Thanks to the skill of the dispositions which were taken and the endurance and heroism of the troops, the peril was averted. This was the last effort of the enemy, who himself had shot his bolt.   In the early days of October the Russians in turn gained a success over the Austrians, and gradually the immense front became fixed and both sides went to ground.

This marked the end of the long retreat which had begun in May.   In spite of all their efforts the Germans had not obtained a decision.   The Russian armies had abandoned a large stretch of territory, but they had everywhere escaped the clutches of their foes.

The Czar returned to Tsarskoïe-Selo on October 6th for a few days, and it was decided that Alexis Nicolaïevitch should go back with him to G.H.Q., for he was most anxious to show the Heir to the troops. The Czarina bowed to this necessity.   She realised how greatly the Czar suffered from loneliness, for at one of the most tragic hours of his life he was deprived of the presence of his family, his greatest consolation.   She knew what a comfort it would be to have his son with him.   Yet her heart bled at the thought of Alexis leaving her.   It was the first time she had been separated from him, and one can imagine what a sacrifice it meant to the mother, who never left her child, even for a few minutes, without wondering anxiously whether she would ever see him alive again.

We left for Mohileff on October 14th, and the Czarina and the Grand-Duchesses came to the station to see us off.   As I

THE CZAR AND CZAREVITCH ON THE BANKS OF THE DNIEPER.
SUMMER OF 1916.

THE CZAR AND CZAREVITCH NEAR MOHILEFF. SUMMER OF 1916.

[Facing page 148.

was saying good-bye to her, Her Majesty asked me to write every day to give her news of her son. I promised to carry out her wishes faithfully the whole time we were away.

The next day we stopped at Riegitza, where the Czar wished to review some troops which had been withdrawn from the front and were billeted in the neighbourhood. All these regiments had taken part in the exhausting campaigns in Galicia and the Carpathians, and their establishment had been almost entirely renewed two or three times over. But in spite of the terrible losses they had suffered, they marched past the Czar with a proud and defiant bearing. Of course, they had been resting behind the line for several weeks, and had had time to recover from their weariness and privations. It was the first time that the Czar had passed any of his troops in review since he had taken over the Command. They now looked upon him both as their Emperor and Generalissimo. After the ceremony he mixed with the men and conversed personally with several of them, asking questions about the severe engagements in which they had taken part. Alexis Nicolaïevitch was at his father's heels, listening intently to the stories of these men, who had so often stared death in the face. His features, which were always expressive, became quite strained in the effort not to lose a single word of what the men were saying. His presence at the Czar's side greatly interested the soldiers, and when he had gone they were heard exchanging in a whisper their ideas about his age, size, looks, etc. But the point that made the greatest impression upon them was the fact that the Czarevitch was wearing the uniform of a private soldier, which had nothing to distinguish it from that of a boy in the service.

On October 16th we arrived at Mohileff, a little White Russian town of a highly provincial appearance to which the

Grand-Duke Nicholas had transferred G.H.Q. during the great German offensive two months before.   The Czar occupied the house of the Governor, which was situated on the summit of the steep left bank of the Dnieper.   He was on the first floor in two fairly large rooms, one of which was his study and the other his bedroom.   He had decided that his son should share his room.   Alexis Nicolaïevitch's   camp-bed was accordingly placed next to his father's.   I myself and some members of the Czar's military suite were lodged in the local court-house, which had been converted for use by G.H.Q.

Our time was spent much as follows.   Every morning at half-past nine the Czar called on the General Staff.   He usually stayed there until one o'clock, and I took advantage of his absence to work with Alexis Nicolaïevitch in his study, which we had been obliged to make our workroom owing to lack of space.   We then took lunch in the main room of the Governor's house.   Every day there were some thirty guests, which included General Alexeieff, his principal assistants, the heads of all the military missions of the Allies, the suite, and a few officers who were passing through Mohileff.   After lunch the Czar dealt with urgent business and then about three we went for a drive in a car.

When we had proceeded a certain distance from the town we stopped and went for a walk in the neighbourhood for an hour.   One of our favourite haunts was the pretty pine-wood in the heart of which is the little village of Saltanovka, where the army of Marshal Davout met the troops of General Raievsky on July 29th, 1912.[1]   On our return the Czar resumed work while Alexis Nicolaïevitch prepared the lessons for the

---

[1] The French army in its march on Moscow occupied Mohileff on July 19th, and Marshal Davout lived for several days in the same house which the Czar and Czarevitch had made their quarters.

next day in his father's study. One day when I was there as usual the Czar turned towards me, pen in hand, and interrupted me in my reading to remark abruptly :

" If anyone had told me that I should one day sign a declaration of war on Bulgaria I should have called him a lunatic. Yet that day has come. But I am signing against my will, as I am certain that the Bulgarian people have been deceived by their king and the partisans of Austria, and that the majority remain friendly to Russia. Race feeling will soon revive and they will realise their mistake, but it will be too late then."

The incident shows what a simple life we led at G.H.Q., and the intimacy which was the result of the extraordinary circumstances under which I was working.

As the Czar was anxious to visit the troops with the Czarevitch, we left for the front on October 24th. The next day we arrived at Berditcheff, where General Ivanoff, commanding the South-Western Front, joined our train. A few hours later we were at Rovno. It was in this town that General Brussiloff had established his headquarters, and we were to accompany him to the place where the troops had been assembled. We went by car, as we had more than twelve miles to cover. As we left the town a squadron of aeroplanes joined us and escorted us until we saw the long grey lines of the units massed behind a forest. A minute later we were among them. The Czar walked down the front of the troops with his son, and then each unit defiled in turn before him. He then had the officers and men on whom decorations were to be bestowed called out of the ranks and gave them the St. George's Cross.

It was dark before the ceremony was over. On our return

the Czar, having heard from General Ivanoff that there was a casualty station quite near, decided to visit it at once. We entered a dark forest and soon perceived a small building feebly lit by the red flames of torches. The Czar and Alexis Nicolaïevitch entered the house, and the Czar went up to all the wounded and questioned them in a kindly way. His unexpected arrival at so late an hour at a spot so close to the front was the cause of the general astonishment which could be read on every face. One private soldier, who had just been bandaged and put back in bed, gazed fixedly at the Czar, and when the latter bent over him he raised his only sound hand to touch his sovereign's clothes and satisfy himself that it was really the Czar who stood before him and not a ghost. Close behind his father stood Alexis Nicolaïevitch, who was deeply moved by the groaning he heard and the suffering he felt all around him.

We rejoined our train and immediately left for the south. When we woke next morning we were in Galicia. During the night we had crossed the former Austrian frontier. The Czar was anxious to congratulate the troops, whose prodigies of valour had enabled them to remain on hostile soil notwithstanding the dearth of arms and ammunition. We left the railway at Bogdanovka and gradually mounted the plateau on which units from all the regiments of General Tcherbatcheff's army had been assembled. When the review was over the Czar disregarded the objections of his suite and visited the Perchersky Regiment, three miles from the front lines, at a place which enemy artillery fire could have reached. We then returned to our cars, which we had left in a forest, and went to General Lechitzsky's army, which was some thirty miles away. We were overtaken by darkness on our way back. A thick mist covered the countryside; we lost our way and twice had to go back. But after many wanderings we at length struck the railway again, though we were sixteen miles from the place where we had left our train! Two hours later we left for G.H.Q.

The Czar brought away a most encouraging impression from his tour of inspection. It was the first time that he had been in really close contact with the troops, and he was glad that he had been able to see with his own eyes, practically in the firing-line, the fine condition of the regiments and the splendid spirit with which they were inspired.

We returned to Mohileff in the evening of October 27th, and the next morning Her Majesty and the Grand-Duchesses also arrived at G.H.Q. During their journey the Czarina and her daughters had stopped at several towns in the Governments of Tver, Pskoff, and Mohileff, in order to visit the military hospitals. They stayed three days with us at Mohileff and then the whole family left for Tsarskoïe-Selo, where the Czar was to spend several days.

I have somewhat lingered over the first journey which the Czar made with his son, and to avoid mere repetition I shall confine myself to a short summary of the visits we paid to the armies in the month of November.

We left Tsarskoïe-Selo on the 9th. On the 10th we were at Reval, where the Czar visited a flotilla of submarines which had just come in. The boats were covered with a thick coating of ice, a sparkling shell for them. There were also two English submarines which had surmounted enormous difficulties in penetrating into the Baltic, and had already succeeded in sinking a certain number of German ships. The Czar bestowed the St. George's Cross on their commanding officers.

During our next day at Riga, which formed a kind of advanced bastion in the German lines, we spent several hours with the splendid regiments of Siberian Rifles, which were regarded as some of the finest troops in the Russian army. Their bearing was magnificent, as they marched past before the Czar, answering his salute with the traditional phrase : " Happy to serve Your Imperial Majesty," followed by a tremendous round of cheers.

A few days later we were at Tiraspol, a little town sixty miles north of Odessa, where the Czar reviewed units from the army of General Tcherbatcheff. After the ceremony the Czar, desiring to know for himself what losses the troops had suffered, asked their commanding officers to order all men who had been in the ranks since the beginning of the campaign to raise their hands. The order was given, and but a very few hands were lifted above those thousands of heads. There were whole companies in which not a man moved. The incident made a very great impression on Alexis Nicolaïevitch. It was the first time that reality had brought home to him the horrors of war in so direct a fashion.

The next day, November 22nd, we went to Reni, a small town on the Danube on the Rumanian frontier. An immense quantity of supplies had been collected there, for it was a base for the river steamers which were engaged in taking food, arms and ammunition to the unfortunate Serbians whom the treachery of Bulgaria had just exposed to an Austro-German invasion.

The following day, near Balta in Podolia, the Czar inspected the famous division of Caucasian cavalry whose regiments had won new laurels in the recent campaign. Among other units were the Kuban and Terek Cossacks, perched high in the saddle

THE CZAR AND THE CZAREVITCH AT A RELIGIOUS SERVICE AT G.H.Q., MOHILEFF.

[Facing page 154.

and wearing the huge fur caps which make them look so fierce. As we started to return, the whole mass of cavalry suddenly moved forward, took station on both sides of the road, broke into a gallop, tearing up the hills, sweeping down the banks of ravines, clearing all obstacles, and thus escorted us to the station in a terrific charge in which men and animals crashed together on the ground while above the *mêlée* rose the raucous yells of the Caucasian mountaineers. It was a spectacle at once magnificent and terrible which revealed all the savage instincts of this primitive race.

We did not return to G.H.Q. until November 26th, after having visited practically the whole of the immense front from the Baltic to the Black Sea.

On December 10th we heard that the Czar was intending to visit the regiments of the Guard which were then on the frontier of Galicia. On the morning of our departure, Thursday, December 16th, Alexis Nicolaïevitch, who had caught cold the previous day and was suffering from a heavy catarrh in the head, began to bleed at the nose as a result of sneezing violently. I summoned Professor Fiodrof,[1] but he could not entirely stop the bleeding. In spite of this accident we started off, as all preparations had been made for the arrival of the Czar. During the night the boy got worse. His temperature had gone up and he was getting weaker. At three o'clock in the morning Professor Fiodrof, alarmed at his responsibilities, decided to have the Czar roused and ask him to return to Mohileff, where he could attend to the Czarevitch under more favourable conditions.

---

[1] Professor Fiodrof accompanied the Czar on all his journeys after the latter took over the supreme command. Dr. Botkin and Dr. Derevenko had remained behind at Tsarskoïe-Selo.

The next morning we were on our way back to G.H.Q., but the boy's state was so alarming that it was decided to take him back to Tsarskoïe-Selo. The Czar called on the General Staff and spent two hours with General Alexeieff. Then he joined us and we started off at once. Our journey was particularly harrowing, as the patient's strength was failing rapidly. We had to have the train stopped several times to be able to change the plugs. Alexis Nicolaïevitch was supported in bed by his sailor Nagorny (he could not be allowed to lie full length), and twice in the night he swooned away and I thought the end had come.

Towards morning there was a slight improvement, however, and the hæmorrhage lessened. At last we reached Tsarskoïe-Selo. It was eleven o'clock. The Czarina, who had been torn with anguish and anxiety, was on the platform with the Grand-Duchesses. With infinite care the invalid was taken to the palace. The doctors ultimately succeeded in cauterizing the scar which had formed at the spot where a little blood-vessel had burst. Once more the Czarina attributed the improvement in her son's condition that morning to the prayers of Rasputin, and she remained convinced that the boy had been saved thanks to his intervention.

The Czar stayed several days with us, but he was anxious to get away as he was wishful to take advantage of the comparative stagnation at the front to visit the troops and get into the closest possible touch with them.

His journeys to the front had been a great success. His presence had everywhere aroused immense enthusiasm, not only among the men but also among the peasants, who swarmed in from the country round whenever his train stopped, in the hope of catching a glimpse of their sovereign. The Czar was

certain that his efforts would tend to revive feelings of patriotism and personal loyalty in the nation and the army.   His
recent experiences persuaded him that he had succeeded, and
those who went with him thought the same.   Was it an
illusion ?   He who denies its truth can know little of the
Russian people, and cannot have the slightest idea how deep-
rooted was monarchical sentiment in the *moujik*.

CHAPTER XIII

THE CZAR AT THE DUMA—THE CAMPAIGN IN GALICIA—OUR LIFE AT G.H.Q.—GROWING DIS-AFFECTION IN THE REAR

(1916)

CHAPTER XIII

THE CZAR AT THE DUMA—THE CAMPAIGN IN GALICIA—OUR LIFE AT G.H.Q.—GROWING DIS-AFFECTION IN THE REAR

(1916)

THE Czar had returned to G.H.Q. alone on December 25th, and three days later he reviewed on the Galician frontier the divisions of the Guard which had been concentrated in view of an imminent offensive. The absence of Alexis Nicolaïevitch was a real sorrow to him, as he had been looking forward eagerly to presenting him to his Guard. He had then returned to Mohileff.

Towards the end of the year 1915 the military situation of the Russians had greatly improved. The army had taken advantage of the quiet months which followed the conclusion of the great German offensive at the end of September, 1915, and, thanks to the enormous reserves in man-power at the disposal of the country, it had easily made good the very heavy losses it had suffered in the retreat. Once more the Germans found themselves baulked of the great prize they had promised themselves—a prize which their brilliant successes at the opening of the campaign seemed to have assured. They had growing doubts about their ability to overcome the stubborn Russian resistance by arms, and by clever propaganda and cunning intrigues they were now endeavouring to stir up such disaffection in the interior of the country as would hasten, they hoped, the consummation so devoutly to be desired. But in the person of the Czar they found an insurmountable obstacle to the realisation of their designs. That obstacle must be removed.

By assuming the command of his troops and thus staking his crown on the struggle, the Czar had definitely deprived his enemies of all hopes of a reconciliation. At Berlin the authorities now knew that Nicholas II. would stand by his allies to the bitter end, and that all attempts at a *rapprochement* would be broken against his unswerving determination to continue the war at any cost. They also knew that the Czar was the sole bond between the different parties in the Empire, and that once it was removed no organised power would be capable of averting dismemberment and anarchy.

The German General Staff therefore devoted itself unceasingly to ruin the prestige of the monarchy and bring about the downfall of the Czar. To attain that object the essential step was to compromise the Czar in the eyes of his people and his allies. Germany had in Russia many sources of intelligence and powerful means of action, and she devoted herself to spreading the idea that the Czar was thinking of liquidating the war and making a separate peace.

The Czar decided to nip these intrigues in the bud and to define his intentions beyond doubt. On January 2nd, at Zamirie, where he was inspecting the regiments of General Kuropatkin's army, he ended his address to the troops with the following formal declaration :

" You need have no fear. As I announced at the beginning of the war, I will not make peace until we have driven the last enemy soldier beyond our frontiers, nor will I conclude peace except by agreement with our allies, to whom we are bound not only by treaties but by sincere friendship and the blood spilt in a common cause."

Nicholas II. thus confirmed in the presence of his army that solemn compact which had been entered upon on August 2nd, 1914, and renewed when he had become Commander-in-Chief of the Russian armies. The Government was anxious to give the widest possible publicity to the Czar's speech, and had it printed and distributed among the armies and in the country districts.

In January and February the Czar continued his visits to the front and G.H.Q. (it was at Mohileff that he spent the Russian New Year), and returned to Tsarskoïe-Selo on February 21st, the day before the opening of the Duma. Five days before, the news of the capture of the fortress of Erzerum, which had so long been the backbone of the Turkish resistance, had caused great joy throughout Russia. It was certainly a fine success, and the offensive of the army of the Caucasus continued to make rapid headway.

The morning after his arrival the Czar carried out his intention of going with his brother, the Grand-Duke Michael, to the Tauride Palace, where the Duma was to resume its labours that day. It was the first time that the representatives of the nation had received a visit from their sovereign, and in political circles great importance was attached to this historical event. It bore witness to the Czar's ardent desire for closer co-operation with the people's representatives, and the step was particularly warmly welcomed, as confidence in the Government had been shaken as the result of the reverses suffered by the army and the crushing charges made against the former Minister of War, General Sukhomlinoff.

The Czar was received on his arrival at the Tauride Palace by M. Rodzianko, President of the Duma, who conducted him into the Catherine Hall, where he was present at a *Te Deum* to celebrate the capture of Erzerum. Then turning to the deputies, the Czar expressed his great pleasure at being among them, and voiced his absolute conviction that in the tragic days through which Russia was passing they would all unite their efforts and work together in perfect harmony for the welfare of the country. His words were received with vociferous cheers.

The Czar withdrew after a visit to the chambers and offices of the Tauride Palace. Half an hour later the President, in opening the session, ended his speech with these words :

" The direct association of the Czar with his people, that benefit which is inestimable and indispensable to the prosperity of the Russian Empire, is now strengthened by a tie which is still more potent. This good news will fill all hearts with joy even in the remotest corners of our land, and give fresh courage to our glorious soldiers, the defenders of their country."

On that memorable day it seemed that the sovereign, the Ministers, and the representatives of the nation had one thought, and one thought alone—to conquer at whatever cost.

The same evening the Czar went to the Council of State, which was also resuming its labours that day. Then he returned to Tsarskoïe-Selo, which he left next morning for G.H.Q. This was the time of the great onslaught on Verdun, and it was essential that Russia should intervene without delay in order to draw a larger portion of the German forces upon herself. It was decided to take the offensive.

The attack was launched about March 15th in the Dvinsk and Vilna sectors, and at first it was crowned with success, but the progress of the Russians was slow, for the Germans offered a very stubborn resistance. There had been a thaw, the roads were almost impracticable, and the men had to wade through mud and marsh. The attack died down about the beginning of April and soon came to a standstill. Yet the diversion had borne fruit, for the Germans had found themselves compelled to send considerable reinforcements to the threatened sectors.

Alexis Nicolaïevitch had remained very weak as the result of the excessive hæmorrhage which had so endangered his life in December. It was February before he was quite strong again, but the Czarina had learned from experience, and intended to keep him at Tsarskoïe-Selo until the return of the fine weather.[1]

I was far from complaining of the Czarina's decision, for the Czarevitch's education was suffering as the result of our long visits to the front.

We did not return to G.H.Q. until May 17th. The Czar was to remain there for a considerable time. A fortnight after our arrival—on June 4th—the great offensive of General Brussiloff opened in Galicia. It was a complete triumph, and our successes were greatly extended in the following days. Under the pressure of the Russian army the Austrian front gave way and was withdrawn towards Lemberg. The number of prisoners was very large, and the situation of the Austrians in

---

[1] I should like to record a slight incident at the beginning of spring when the Czar was at Tsarskoïe-Selo between his visits to the front. It illustrates the kind of feelings the Czar entertained for Germany and tried to instil into his son. The Czarevitch was playing in the park that day, and the Czar and the Grand-Duchesses were also there. He slipped behind his youngest sister, who had not seen him coming, and threw a huge snowball at her. His father had witnessed the act. He called the boy to him and talked to him severely. "You ought to be ashamed of yourself, Alexis! You're behaving like a German, to attack anyone from behind when they can't defend themselves. It's horrid and cowardly. Leave that sort of behaviour to the Germans!"

the Lutzk sector became highly critical. The news of this fine victory was received with immense enthusiasm at G.H.Q. It was to be the last cause of rejoicing for the Czar.

Since our return to Headquarters our life had followed the same course as during our previous visits, though I no longer gave the Czarevitch his lessons in his father's study, but in a little verandah which we had converted into a schoolroom or in a large tent in the garden, which was also our dining-room. It was here that the Czar took his meals after the hot weather began. We took advantage of the fine summer days to go sailing on the Dnieper. We had the use of a small yacht which had been placed at our disposal by the Ministry of Ways and Communications.

From time to time the Czarina and the Grand-Duchesses paid short visits to G.H.Q. They lived in their train, but joined the Czar at lunch and came with us on our excursions. The Czar in return dined with the Czarina and spent part of the evening with his family whenever he could. The Grand-Duchesses greatly enjoyed these visits to Mohileff—all too short to their taste—which meant a little change in their monotonous and austere lives. They had far more freedom here than at Tsarskoïe-Selo. As is so often the case in Russia, the station at Mohileff was a very long way from the town and almost in the open country. The Grand-Duchesses spent their spare time visiting the peasants of the neighbourhood or the families of railway employees. Their simple ways and natural kindness soon won all hearts, and as they adored children you could see them always accompanied by a mob of ragamuffins collected on their walks and duly stuffed with sweets.

Unfortunately, life at Mohileff grievously interrupted Alexis

THREE OF THE GRAND-DUCHESSES (OLGA, ANASTASIE, AND TATIANA) VISITING THE WIFE AND CHILDREN OF A RAILWAY EMPLOYEE AT MOHILEFF.

THE CZARINA AND THE GRAND-DUCHESS TATIANA TALKING TO REFUGEES. MOHILEFF, MAY, 1916.

[*Facing page* 166.

Nicolaïevitch's studies and was also bad for his health. The impressions he gained there were too numerous and exciting for so delicate a nature as his. He became nervous, fretful, and incapable of useful work. I told the Czar what I thought. He admitted that my objections were well founded, but suggested that these drawbacks were compensated for by the fact that his son was losing his timidity and natural wildness, and that the sight of all the misery he had witnessed would give him a salutary horror of war for the rest of his life.

But the longer we stayed at the front the stronger was my conviction that it was doing the Czarevitch a lot of harm. My position was becoming difficult, and on two or three occasions I had to take strong steps with the boy. I had an idea that the Czar did not entirely approve, and did not back me up as much as he might have done. As I was extremely tired by my work in the last three years—I had had no holiday since September, 1913—I decided to ask for a few weeks' leave. My colleague, M. Petroff, came to take my place, and I left General Headquarters on July 14th.

As soon as I arrived at Tsarskoïe-Selo the Czarina summoned me, and I had a long talk with her, in the course of which I tried to show the grave disadvantages for Alexis Nicolaïevitch of his long visits to the front. She replied that the Czar and herself quite realised them, but thought that it was better to sacrifice their son's education temporarily, even at the risk of injuring his health, than to deprive him of the other benefits he was deriving from his stay at Mohileff. With a candour which utterly amazed me she said that all his life the Czar had suffered terribly from his natural timidity and from the fact that as he had been kept too much in the background he had found himself badly prepared for the duties

of a ruler on the sudden death of Alexander III. The Czar
had vowed to avoid the same mistakes in the education of his
son.

I realised that I had come up against a considered decision,
and was not likely to secure any modification. All the same,
it was agreed that Alexis Nicolaïevitch's lessons should be
resumed on a more regular plan at the end of September, and
that I should receive some assistance in my work.

When our conversation was over the Czarina made me stay
behind to dinner. I was the only guest that evening. After
the meal we went out on the terrace. It was a beautiful
summer evening, warm and still. Her Majesty was stretched
on a sofa, and she and two of her daughters were knitting
woollen clothing for the soldiers. The two other Grand-
Duchesses were sewing. Alexis Nicolaïevitch was naturally
the principal topic of conversation. They never tired of
asking me what he did and said. I spent an hour thus in this
homely and quiet circle, suddenly introduced into the intimacy of that family life which etiquette had forbidden me
from entering, save in this casual and rare fashion.

In the days following I spent my time in a round of visits
and renewing relationships which my journeys to the front had
compelled me to neglect. I thus saw people in different strata
of society in the capital, and was not slow to realise that far-
reaching changes had taken place in public opinion in recent
months. People did not confine themselves to violent attacks
on the Government, but went on to attack the person of the
Czar.

Since that memorable February 22nd on which Nicholas II.
had presented himself to the Duma in his sincere desire for

reconciliation, the differences between the sovereign and the representatives of the nation had only increased. The Czar had long been hesitating to grant the liberal concessions which had been demanded. He considered it was the wrong time, and that it was dangerous to attempt reforms while the war was raging. It was not that he clung to his autocratic personal prerogatives, for he was simplicity and modesty itself, but he feared the effect such radical changes might have at so critical a moment. When the Czar declared on February 22nd that he was happy to be among the representatives of his people, the Czar had spoken his real thoughts. In inviting them to unite all their efforts for the welfare of the country in the tragic days through which it was passing, he was urging them to forget all their political differences and have only one goal—victory and belief in their Czar until the end of the war.

Why did he not make a solemn promise that day to give the nation the liberties they asked as soon as circumstances permitted? Why did he not try to recover by his acts that confidence of the Duma which he felt he was losing? The answer is that those around him had made it impossible for him to find out for himself what was really going on in the country.

The Czar's visit to the Tauride Palace had given rise to great hopes. They had not been fulfilled, and men were not slow to see that nothing had been changed. The conflict with the Government was immediately resumed. The demands became more pressing and recrimination more violent. Frightened by the false reports of those who abused his confidence, the Czar began to regard the opposition of the Duma as the result of revolutionary agitation, and thought he could re-establish his authority by measures which only swelled the general discontent.

But it was the Czarina who was the special object of attack. The worst insinuations about her conduct had gained currency and were believed even by circles which hitherto had rejected them with scorn. As I have said, the presence of Rasputin at Court was a growing blot on the prestige of the sovereigns, and gave rise to the most malicious comments. It was not as if the critics confined themselves to attacks upon the private life of the Czarina. She was openly accused of Germanophile sympathies, and it was suggested that her feelings for Germany could become a danger to the country. The word " treason " was not yet heard, but guarded hints showed that the suspicion had been planted in a good many heads. I knew that all this was the result of German pro-paganda and intrigues.[1]

I have explained above that in the autumn of 1915 the Berlin Government had realised that they could never over-throw Russia as long as she stood united round her Czar, and that from that moment her one idea had been to provoke a revolution which would involve the fall of Nicholas II. In view of the difficulties of attacking the Czar directly, the Germans had concentrated their efforts against the Czarina and begun a subterranean campaign of defamation against her. It was skilfully planned and began to show results before long. They had stopped at nothing in the way of calumny. They

---

[1] I was able to ascertain this for myself at the end of 1915. At the house of some friends one day I met a young officer whose political opinions were favourable to the Court. He told us with intense indignation that on the Czarina's orders someone had taken gifts and money to the German officers being treated at the same hospital as he had been in. This envoy had not even entered the rooms occupied by the Russian officers. Astonished at his story, I asked for details. An enquiry was ordered. It completely confirmed the story I had been told, but it was impossible to trace the individual who had succeeded, by the use of forged papers, in making the authorities believe he had an official mission. Pure chance had brought me into contact with one of the many provocations organised by German spies with German money.

had adopted the classic procedure, so well known to history, of striking the monarch in the person of his consort. It is, of course, always easier to damage the reputation of a woman, especially when she is a foreigner. Realising all the advantages to be derived from the fact that the Czarina was a German princess, they had endeavoured to suggest very cunningly that she was a traitor to Russia. It was the best method of compromising her in the eyes of the nation. The accusation had been favourably received in certain quarters in Russia and had become a formidable weapon against the dynasty.

The Czarina knew all about the campaign in progress against her and it pained her as a most profound injustice, for she had accepted her new country, as she had adopted her new faith, with all the fervour of her nature. She was Russian by sentiment as she was orthodox by conviction.[1]

My residence behind the front also enabled me to realise how much the country was suffering from the war. The weariness and privations were causing general discontent. As a result of the increasing shortage of rolling-stock, fuel, which had been cruelly scarce in the winter, continued to be

---

[1] At the time I am writing I find what I have said fully confirmed in the following passage from an article by M. Paleologue, French Ambassador at Petrograd : *La Russie des Tsars pendant la Grande Guerre* (*Revue des Deux Mondes* of March 15th, 1921) :

" I have several times heard the Czarina charged with having preserved sympathies, predilections, and a warm corner for Germany when she was on the throne. The unfortunate woman in no way merited these strictures, which she knew of and made her so unhappy. Alexandra Feodorovna was German neither in spirit nor in sentiment. She never was."

Further on he says :

" Her education, bringing-up, her intellectual and moral outlook were entirely English. She was English in appearance and bearing, in a certain element of reserve and Puritanism, in the intractable and militant austerity of her conscience, and, lastly, in many of her personal habits. In any case, that was all that was left of her Western origin. The basis of her character had become entirely Russian. In spite of the hostile legend which was growing up round her name, I did not doubt her patriotism. She had a fervent love of Russia."

unpurchasable. It was the same with food, and the cost of living continued to rise at an alarming rate.

On August 11th I returned to G.H.Q. thoroughly perturbed at all I had seen and heard. It was pleasant to find the atmosphere at Mohileff very different from that at Petrograd, and to feel the stimulating influence of circles which offered so stern a resistance to the " defeatist " spirit at work at home. Yet the authorities there were very concerned at the political situation, although that was not so obvious at first sight.

Alexis Nicolaïevitch gave me a very affectionate welcome when I came back (he had written to me regularly while I was away), and the Czar received me with exceptional kindness. I could thus congratulate myself on the result of leaving my pupil for some time, especially as it might have been a false step, and I took up my duties again with renewed energies. My English colleague, Mr. Gibbes, had meanwhile joined us, and as M. Petroff remained with us, the Czarevitch's lessons could proceed practically regularly.

At the front the fighting had gradually died down in the northern and central sectors. It continued only in Galicia, where the Russians were still driving the Austrians before them, and their defeat would long since have become a flight if they had not been supported by a large number of German regiments.

The campaign of 1916, however, had convinced the Russian General Staff that they would never break the resistance of the enemy and secure final victory so long as they suffered from so great a lack of artillery. Their inferiority in that respect prevented a thorough exploitation of the successes gained by the courage of the troops and their numerical superiority at the beginning of each attack. There was nothing for it but to wait until the material promised by the Allies, the delivery of which had been delayed by difficulties of transport, was ready and available.

The Austrian defeats had had a very great effect on Rumania. She was more and more inclined to associate herself with the cause of the Entente, but she was still hesitating to enter the arena. The Russian Minister at Bucharest had had to bring strong pressure to bear to induce her to make up her mind.[1]

On August 27th Rumania at length declared war. Her position was very difficult, as she was on the extreme left flank of the immense Russian front, from which she was separated by the Carpathians. She was threatened with an Austro-German attack from the north and west, and could be taken in rear by the Bulgarians. That is exactly what happened, and the beginning of October marked the beginning of the reverses which were to end only with the occupation of almost the whole of Rumania.

[1]As soon as the danger was apparent the Russian General Staff had taken steps to send help to the Rumanian army, but the distances were great and the communications extremely defective. Nor was Russia in a position to reduce the effectives on her own front to any serious degree, for in case of urgent necessity she would have found herself unable to retrieve the divisions sent to Rumania in time. Under pressure from the Czar, however, all the available reinforcements had been directed there. The question was whether these troops would arrive in time to save Bucharest.

---

[1] It was only subsequently that I learned that, to overcome the resistance he met with at Bucharest, the Minister for Foreign Affairs, Sturmer (who had succeeded Sazonoff), had promised that Russian troops would be sent to Rumania. He had not referred to G.H.Q. first.

We returned to Tsarskoïe-Selo on November 1st. The impression made by the Rumanian disaster had been great, and the Minister for Foreign Affairs had been held responsible. At the beginning of the year Sturmer had succeeded Goremykin as President of the Council of Ministers. His appointment had been badly received, and he had simply made one fault after another. It had been as the result of his intrigues that Sazonoff, who had rendered such great services as Foreign Minister, had had to resign, and Sturmer had hastened to take his place while remaining President of the Council.

He was hated as much for his name as his acts. It was alleged that he only kept himself in power thanks to the influence of Rasputin. Some even went so far as to accuse him of pro-German sympathies, and to suspect him of favouring a separate peace with Germany.[1] Nicholas II. compromised himself by keeping for so long a Minister whom all suspected. It was hoped that the Czar would ultimately realise that he had been deceived once more, but we all feared that he would find out only too late, when the harm done was irremediable.[2]

---

[1] History will one day settle what part Sturmer played. If he did not actually work for a *rapprochement* with Germany, though everything seems to show that he did, he none the less did his country irreparable harm through his criminal negligence and utter lack of scruples.

[2] The very education of a sovereign makes him entirely unfitted for the task before him, and yet it is impossible to make good the defect afterwards. The larger the part he plays in government the less he knows of what is going on. To keep him away from his people he is given nothing but mutilated, distorted, and "cooked" reports. No one can realise the resisting power of those about a throne, the invincible apathy of a bureaucracy steeped in traditional observance and routine ! Whatever strength of mind, whatever tenacity a sovereign may display in finding out the truth, does he ever really succeed ? Napoleon had been through the school of life, and raised himself to a throne by sheer genius and audacity, but his fate was the same as that of other rulers. In the last years of his reign did he still know what was happening in France ? Had he still a sense of reality ?

CHAPTER XIV

POLITICAL TENSION—THE DEATH OF RASPUTIN
(DECEMBER, 1916)

CHAPTER XIV

POLITICAL TENSION—THE DEATH OF RASPUTIN
(DECEMBER, 1916)

THE political atmosphere became more and more heavy, and we could feel the approach of the storm. Discontent had become so general that in spite of the censorship the Press began to speak about it. Party feeling ran ever higher, and there was only one point on which opinion was unanimous—the necessity of putting an end to the omnipotence of Rasputin. Everyone regarded him as the evil counsellor of the Court and held him responsible for all the disasters from which the country was suffering. He was accused of every form of vice and debauchery and denounced as a vile and loathsome creature of fantastic habits, and capable of baseness and ignominy of every kind. To many he was an emanation of the devil himself, the anti-Christ whose dreaded coming was to be the signal for the worst calamities.

The Czar had resisted the influence of Rasputin for a long time. At the beginning he had tolerated him because he dare not weaken the Czarina's faith in him—a faith which kept her alive. He did not like to send him away, for if Alexis Nicolaïevitch had died, in the eyes of the mother he would have been the murderer of his own son. Yet he had maintained a cautious reserve, and had only gradually been won over to the views of

his wife.   Many attempts had been made to enlighten him as to
the true character of Rasputin and secure his dismissal.   His
confidence had been shaken, but the Czar had never yet been
convinced.[1]

On November 6th we left Tsarskoïe-Selo, and after a short
stay at Mohileff we left on the 9th for Kieff, where the Czar was
to visit the Dowager Empress.   He stayed two days in the
company of his mother and some of his relations, who did their
best to show him how serious the situation was and persuade
him to remedy it by energetic measures.   The Czar was greatly
influenced by the advice which was given him.   He had never
seemed to me so worried before.   He was usually very self-
controlled, but on this occasion he showed himself nervous
and irritable, and once or twice he spoke roughly to Alexis
Nicolaïevitch.

We returned to G.H.Q. on the 12th, and a few days later
Sturmer fell, to the unconcealed relief of everyone.   The Czar
entrusted the office of President of the Council to A. Trepoff,
who was known as an advocate of moderate and sane reforms.
Hope revived.   Unfortunately the intrigues continued.   The
Germans flattered themselves that these were only the prelude
to grave troubles and redoubled their efforts, sowing the seeds
of doubt and suspicion everywhere and trying to compromise
the Court beyond repair in the eyes of the nation.

Trepoff had asked the Czar to dismiss the Minister of the
Interior, Protopopoff, whose utter inefficiency and the fact
that he was a disciple of Rasputin had made him bitterly

---

[1] It really seems that a perverse fate intervened to protect Rasputin.
One day the Czar was given a document in which the excesses of the *staretz*
were set forth highly circumstantially.   In reading it the Czar observed that
on the day and hour at which one of the acts mentioned in the document
were alleged to have taken place Rasputin had actually been at Tsarskoïe-
Selo.   Nothing more was required to convince the Czar that the whole report
was simply a tissue of lies.

unpopular. The President of the Council felt that he would never be able to do anything useful so long as that Minister remained at his post, for all the politicians of any standing proclaimed their helplessness and were refusing to accept responsibility.

The courageous initiative of patriots such as Sazonoff, Krivoshin, Samarin, Ignatieff, and A. Trepoff—to mention but a few—was not supported as it might have been. If the intelligent masses of the nation had grouped themselves round them the growing peril could have been averted and in quite legal fashion. But these men did not receive the support they were entitled to expect. Criticism and the intrigues and rivalries of individuals and parties prevented that unity which alone could have saved the situation.

If unity had been realised it would have represented a power such as would have paralysed the evil influence of Rasputin and his adherents. Unfortunately those who did realise it were the exception. The majority kept out of a disagreeable conflict, and by retiring from the field left it free to adventurers and the apostles of intrigue. They made no effort to lighten the burden of the men who realised the danger and had undertaken to save the Czar, in spite of himself, and to support the tottering régime until the end of the war.

The Czar had originally acquiesced in Trepoff's suggestion, but under the influence of the Czarina he had changed his mind and remained irresolute, not knowing what to decide. He had been deceived so often that he did not know in whom he could have confidence. He felt himself alone and deserted by all. He had spent himself without reflection since he had assumed the Supreme Command, but the burden he had taken upon his shoulders was too heavy and beyond his strength. He realised the fact himself. Hence his weakness towards the Czarina, and the fact that he tended more and more to yield to her will.

Yet many of the decisions he had taken in 1915 and his visit to the Duma in February, 1916, show that till then, at any rate, he could resist her when he was sure that it was for the good of the country. It was only in the autumn of 1916 that he succumbed to her influence, and then only because he was worn out by the strain of his double functions as Czar and Commander-in-Chief, and in his increasing isolation he did not know what to do to escape a situation which was getting worse from day to day. If he had received better support at that time from the moderate parties, who can say that he would not have found the strength to continue his resistance !

The Czarina herself sincerely believed—on the strength of Rasputin's word—that Protopopoff was the man who could save Russia. He was kept in office, and Trepoff, realising his impotence, lost no time in resigning his post.

We returned to Tsarskoïe-Selo on December 8th. The situation was becoming more strained every day. Rasputin knew that the storm of hatred was gathering against him, and dare not leave the little flat he occupied in Petrograd. Exasperation with him had reached fever-heat, and the country was waiting for deliverance and fervently hoping that someone would remove the man who was considered the evil genius of Russia. But Rasputin was well guarded. He had the protection of the Imperial police, who watched over his house night and day. He had also the protection of the Revolutionary Socialists, who realised that he was working for them.

I do not think that Rasputin was an agent—in the usual sense of the word—in Germany's pay, but he was certainly a formidable weapon in the hands of the German General Staff, which was vitally interested in the prolongation of the life of so valuable an ally and had surrounded him with spies who were also guards. The Germans had found him a splendid weapon for compromising the Court, and had made great use of him.

Many attempts had been made, even by the Czarina's greatest friends at Court, to open her eyes to the true character of Rasputin. They had all collapsed against the blind faith she had in him. But in this tragic hour the Grand-Duchess Elizabeth Feodorovna[1] wished to make one last effort to save her sister. She came from Moscow, intending to spend a few days at Tsarskoïe-Selo with the relations she loved so dearly. She was nine years older than her sister, and felt an almost maternal tenderness for her. It was at her house, it will be remembered, that the young princess had stayed on her first visit to Russia. It was she who had helped Alexandra Feodorovna with wise advice and surrounded her with every attention when she started her reign. She had often tried to open her sister's eyes before, but in vain. Yet this time she hoped that God would give her the powers of persuasion which had hitherto failed her, and enable her to avert the terrible catastrophe she felt was imminent.

As soon as she arrived at Tsarskoïe-Selo she spoke to the Czarina, trying with all the love she bore her to convince her of her blindness, and pleading with her to listen to her warnings for the sake of her family and her country.

The Czarina's confidence was not to be shaken. She realised the feelings which had impelled her sister to take this step, but she was terribly grieved to find her accepting the lying stories of those who desired to ruin the *staretz*, and she

---

[1] The Grand-Duchess Elizabeth Feodorovna had founded a small religious community, of which she was the Superior, at Moscow. She lived there retired from the world, devoting all her time to prayer and good works.

asked her never to mention the subject again.   As the Grand-Duchess persisted, the Czarina broke off the conversation.   The interview was then objectless.

A few hours later the Grand-Duchess left for Moscow, death in her heart.   The Czarina and her daughters accompanied her to the station.   The two sisters took leave of each other.   The tender affection which had associated them since their childhood was still intact, but they realised that there was a broken something lying between them.[1]

They were never to see each other again.

On December 18th we left for Mohileff again.   The situation there had taken a turn for the worse.   The news of the capture of Bucharest had just come in to depress everyone's spirits.   It seemed to justify the most gloomy forebodings.   Rumania appeared to be lost.

We were all oppressed and uneasy, a prey to that vague anxiety which men experience at the approach of some danger or catastrophe.   The muttering of the gathering storm could be heard.

Suddenly the news of Rasputin's death fell like a thunder-bolt.[2]   It was December 31st, and the same day we left for Tsarskoïe-Selo.

---

[1] I had all these details from the lips of Mlle. Schneider, reader to the Czarina, who had once been in the household of the Grand-Duchess Elizabeth, who had always remained very fond of her.

[2] The circumstances of Rasputin's death are to be found in the newspapers of the time.   I will briefly recapitulate them here.   His death was the result of a plot in which some of the participants were the Grand-Duke Dimitri Pavlovitch, first cousin of the Czar, Prince Yussoupoff, whose wife was the niece of Nicholas II., M. Purichkevitch, a monarchist deputy in the Duma, and Dr. Lazarevsky, who accompanied him.   The Grand-Duke wished to show by his presence that it was not a case of an act of rebellion against the Czar, but merely the execution of a miscreant whom the nation had judged and found guilty of abusing the confidence of his sovereign.

Rasputin was killed on the night of December 30th.   Prince Yussoupoff had gone to fetch him in his car very late in the evening, and brought him to his house.   They first tried to poison him, but as the poison was slow in taking effect, Prince Yussoupoff and the deputy killed him with revolvers.   His corpse was thrown into the Neva and was picked up two days later.

I shall never forget what I felt when I saw the Czarina again. Her agonised features betrayed, in spite of all her efforts, how terribly she was suffering. Her grief was inconsolable. Her idol had been shattered. He who alone could save her son had been slain. Now that he had gone, any misfortune, any catastrophe, was possible. The period of waiting began—that dreadful waiting for the disaster which there was no escaping. . . .

CHAPTER XV

THE REVOLUTION—THE ABDICATION OF NICHOLAS II.
(MARCH, 1917)

CHAPTER XV

THE REVOLUTION—THE ABDICATION OF NICHOLAS II
(MARCH, 1917)

RASPUTIN was no more and the nation was avenged. A few brave men had taken upon themselves to secure the disappearance of the man who was execrated by one and all. [1] It might be hoped that after this explosion of wrath faction would die down. Unfortunately it was not so. On the contrary, the struggle between the Czar and the Duma became more bitter than ever.

The Czar was convinced that in existing circumstances all concessions on his part would be regarded as a sign of weakness which, without removing the causes of the discontent which resulted from the miseries and privations of the war, could only diminish his authority and possibly accelerate a revolution. The opposition of the Duma revealed the incapacity and impotence of the Government and in no way improved the situation. Faction became more intense, intrigue multiplied

---

[1] I am referring, of course, to the articulate portion of the nation. The untutored masses cared nothing about him, and among those who knew of his existence a large number were favourable to him. Many considered his death an act of vengeance on the part of the courtiers who were jealous of their privileges. "The first time that one of ourselves gets to the Czar, he is killed by the courtiers," they said.

To the *moujik* the great criminals were those who came between the sovereign and his people, and prevented him from extending his favours to them. There was a popular saying that "the Czar gives, but his servants withhold," in which the peasant expressed his faith in the goodness of his Czar and his hatred of those around him.

at a time when nothing but the presentation of a united front by all the intelligent classes of the nation could have paralysed the evil influence of Protopopoff. A universal effort would have been required to avert the catastrophe which was rapidly approaching. It was true that this meant asking the upper classes to prove that they could show as much self-denial as enlightened patriotism, but in the tragic circumstances through which the country was passing such action might have been expected of them.

How is it that in Russia no one realised what everyone in Germany knew—that a revolution would inevitably deliver up the country to its enemies? " I had often dreamed," writes Ludendorff in his *War Memories,* " of the realisation of that Russian revolution which was to lighten our military burden. A perpetual illusion ! We had the revolution to-day quite unexpectedly. I felt as if a great weight had fallen from my shoulders." [1]

The Germans were the only people in Europe who knew Russia. Their knowledge of it was fuller and more exact than that of the Russians themselves. They had known for a long time that the Czarist régime, with all its faults, was the only one capable of prolonging the Russian resistance. They knew that with the fall of the Czar Russia would be at their mercy. They stopped at nothing to procure his fall. That is why the preservation of the existing system should have been secured at any cost. The revolution was inevitable at that moment, it was said. It could only be averted by the immediate grant of a constitution. And so on ! The fact is

---

[1] Ludendorff, *My War Memories,* vol. ii. (Hutchinson and Co., London). What Ludendorff did not mention, and for good reason, was the untiring efforts Germany had made to produce this revolution which had broken out so unexpectedly.

that the perverse fate which had blinded the sovereigns was to blind the nation in turn.

Yet the Czar was inspired by two dominant sentiments—his political enemies themselves knew it—to which all Russia could rally. One of them was his love for his country and the other his absolute determination to continue the war to the bitter end. In the universal blindness which was the result of party passion men did not realise that, in spite of all, a Czar pledged to the cause of victory was an immense moral asset for the Russian people. They did not see that a Czar who was what he was popularly supposed to be could alone lead the country to victory and save it from bondage to Germany.

The position of the Czar was extraordinarily difficult. To the Extremists of the Right, who regarded a compromise with Germany as their only road to salvation, he was the insurmountable obstacle, who had to make way for another sovereign. To the Extremists of the Left who desired victory, but a victory without a Czar, he was the obstacle which the revolution would remove. And while the latter were endeavouring to undermine the foundations of the monarchy by intensive propaganda at and behind the front—thus playing Germany's game—the moderate parties adopted that most dangerous and yet characteristically Russian course of doing nothing. They were victims of that Slav fatalism which means waiting on events and hoping that some providential force will come and guide them for the public good. They confined themselves to passive resistance because they failed to realise that in so acting they were paralysing the nation.

The general public had unconsciously become the docile tool of German intrigue. The most alarming rumours, accepted and given the widest currency, created an anti-monarchist and defeatist atmosphere behind the front—an atmosphere of distrust and suspicion which was bound to have a speedy effect upon the men in the firing-line themselves. Everyone hacked at the central pillar of the tottering political edifice, and no one thought of attempting to shore it up while still there was time. Everything was done to accelerate the revolution ; nothing to avert its consequences.

It was forgotten that Russia did not consist merely of fifteen to twenty million human beings ripe for parliamentary government, but that it had one hundred and twenty to one hundred and thirty million peasants, most of them rude and uneducated, to whom the Czar was still the Lord's Anointed, he whom God had chosen to direct the destinies of Great Russia. Accustomed from his earliest youth to hear the priest invoke the name of the Czar in the offertory, one of the most solemn moments in the Orthodox liturgy, the *moujik* in his mystical exaltation was bound to attribute to him a character semi-divine.[1]

The Czar was not the head of the Russian Church. He was its protector and defender. But after Peter the Great abolished the patriarchate the people were inclined to regard him as the incarnation of both spiritual and temporal authority. It was an error, of course, but it survived. It was this double aspect of the person of the sovereign which made Czarism mean so much to the masses, and as the Russian people are essentially mystic, the second factor was not a whit less important than the first. For in the mind of the *moujik*, autocracy.could not be separated from Orthodoxy.

The Russian revolution could not be exclusively a political

---

[1] Is not this idea illustrated in the popular saying which betrays the simple faith of the Russian peasant and his feeling of impotence : " God is a very long way up ; the Czar a very long way off "

revolution. It must necessarily have a religious character. When the old system fell it was bound to create such a void in the political and religious conscience of the Russian people that unless care were taken it would involve the whole of the social organism in its fall. To the humble peasant the Czar was both the incarnation of his mystic aspirations and in a sense a tangible reality, impossible to replace by a political formula, which would be an incomprehensible abstraction to him. Into the vacuum created by the collapse of the Czaristic régime the Russian revolution—in view of the passion of the absolute and the proneness to extremes which are characteristic of the Slav nature—was certain to hurl itself with a violence that no government could control. There was a fatal risk that it would all end in political and religious chaos or sheer anarchy.

As the revolution was desired, preparations should have been made to avert this eventuality. Even in times of peace it would have been a formidable risk : to venture upon such a step in war was simply criminal. We Westerners are apt to judge Russian affairs by the governing classes with which we have come in contact—classes which have attained a degree of culture and civilisation equal to our own. We too often forget the millions of semi-barbarous and ignorant beings who understand the simplest and most primitive sentiments alone. Of these the Czarist fetish was one of the most striking examples.

The British Ambassador, getting his information from Russian politicians whose patriotism was above suspicion, but who saw their country as they wanted it to be and not as it really was, allowed himself to be led astray. Insufficient account was taken of the special conditions which made Russia a religious, political, and social anachronism to which none of the formulæ or panaceas of Western Europe would apply. They forgot that in any country at war the early stages of a revolution almost always produce a weakening of the national effort and adversely affect the fighting power of the army. In a country like Russia this would be true to a far greater extent. The Entente made a mistake[1] in thinking that the movement which the beginning of February, 1917, revealed was of popular origin. It was nothing of the kind, and only the governing classes participated in it. The great masses stood aloof. It is not true that it was a fundamental upheaval which overturned the monarchy. It was the fall of the monarchy itself which raised that formidable wave which engulfed Russia and nearly submerged the neighbouring states.

After his return from G.H.Q. the Czar had remained at Tsarskoïe-Selo for the months of January and February. He felt that the political situation was more and more strained, but he had not yet lost all hope. The country was suffering : it was tired of the war and anxiously longing for peace. The opposition was growing from day to day, and the storm was

---

[1] Ludendorff exaggerates the *rôle* of the Entente in the Russian Revolution when he writes : " In March, 1917, a Revolution, the work of the Entente, overthrew the Czar." The movement was supported by the Allies, but it was not their work. Ludendorff shows well enough what were its immediate results for Germany. " The Revolution meant a fatal loss of military power to Russia, weakened the Entente and gave us considerable relief in our heavy task. The General Staff could at once effect important economies of troops and ammunition, and could also exchange divisions on a much greater scale." And further on : " In April and May, 1917, it was the Russian Revolution which saved us in spite of our victory on the Aisne and in Champagne." (Ludendorff, *My War Memories*, vol. ii.).

Thus, by the admission of the Germans themselves, if there had been no Russian Revolution the war would have ended in the autumn of 1917 and millions of human lives would have been spared. Do we realise what would have been the force of a treaty of Versailles signed by the Entente, including Russia ! Germany, seized in a vice, would not have been able to escape the fate of the vanquished. The consequences of the Russian Revolution (Bolshevism) have thrown Russia into the arms of Germany. She is still there. Germany alone is in a position to organise and exploit her immense resources. It is in Russia that Germany is preparing her revenge against the Entente.

threatening, but in spite of everything Nicholas II. hoped that patriotic feeling would carry the day against the pessimism which the trials and worries of the moment made general, and that no one would risk compromising the results of a war which had cost the nation so much by rash and imprudent action.

His faith in his army was also unshaken. He knew that the material sent from France and England was arriving satisfactorily and would improve the conditions under which it had to fight. He had the greatest hopes of the new formations which had been created in the course of the winter.[1] He was certain that his army would be ready in the spring to join in that great offensive of the Allies which would deal Germany her death-blow and thus save Russia : a few weeks more and victory would be his.

Yet the Czar hesitated to leave Tsarskoïe-Selo, such was his anxiety about the political situation. On the other hand, he considered that his departure could not be deferred much longer, and that it was his duty to return to G.H.Q. He ultimately left for Mohileff on Thursday, March 8th, arriving there next morning.

He had hardly left the capital before the first symptoms of insurrection began to be observable in the working-class quarters. The factories went on strike, and the movement spread rapidly during the days following. The population of Petrograd had suffered great privations during the winter, for owing to the shortage of rolling-stock the transport of food and fuel had become very difficult, and there was no sign of improvement in this respect. The Government could think of nothing likely to calm the excitement, and Protopopoff merely

---

[1] Russia had been engaged in a reorganisation of the army which increased the number of her divisions and greatly augmented her striking force.

N

exasperated everyone by the measures of repression—as stupid as criminal—taken by the police. Troops also had been employed. All the regiments being at the front, the only troops at Petrograd were units under instruction, whose loyalty had been thoroughly undermined by organised propaganda in the barracks in spite of counter-measures. There were cases of defection, and after three days of half-hearted resistance unit after unit went over to the insurgents. By the 13th the city was almost entirely in the hands of the revolutionaries, and the Duma proceeded to form a provisional government.

At first we at Mohileff had no idea of the scale of the events which had occurred at Petrograd. Yet after Saturday, March 10th, General Alexeieff and some officers of the Czar's suite had tried to open his eyes and persuade him to grant the liberties the nation demanded immediately. But once more Nicholas II. was deceived by the intentionally incomplete and inaccurate statements of a few ignorant individuals in his suite[1] and would not take their advice.

By the 12th it was impossible to conceal the truth from the Czar any longer ; he understood that extraordinary measures were required, and decided to return to Tsarskoïe-Selo at once.

The Imperial train left Mohileff on the night of the 12th, but on arriving at the station of Malaia-Vichera twenty-four hours later it was ascertained that the station of Tosno, thirty miles south of Petrograd, was in the hands of the insurgents, and that it was impossible to get to Tsarskoïe-Selo. There was nothing for it but to turn back.

---

[1] Professor Fiodorof, realising that every hour's delay meant less chance of averting imminent disaster, went to find General V——, who was one of the most prominent members of the Czar's staff. He found him perched on a ladder engaged in fixing a nail in the wall on which to hang a picture. Fiodorof told him his fears and begged him to see the Czar at once. But the General called him a "revolution maniac," and, picking up his hammer, continued the operation which had been interrupted by his tiresome visitor.

The Czar decided to go to Pskoff to General Russky, the Commander-in-Chief of the Northern Front. He arrived there on the evening of the 14th. When the General had told him the latest developments in Petrograd the Czar instructed him to inform M. Rodzianko by telephone that he was ready to make every concession if the Duma thought that it would tranquillise the nation. The reply came: "It is too late."

Was it really so? The revolutionary movement was confined to Petrograd and its suburbs; in spite of propaganda, the Czar still enjoyed considerable prestige in the army, and his authority with the peasants was intact. Would not the grant of a Constitution and the help of the Duma have been enough to restore to Nicholas II. the popularity he had enjoyed at the beginning of the war?

The reply of the Duma left the Czar with the alternatives of abdicating or marching on Petrograd with the troops which remained faithful to him: the latter would mean civil war in the presence of the enemy. Nicholas II. did not hesitate, and on the morning of the 15th he handed General Russky a telegram informing the President of the Duma that he intended to abdicate in favour of his son.

A few hours later he summoned Professor Fiodorof to his carriage and said:

" Tell me frankly, Sergius Petrovitch. Is Alexis's malady incurable? "

Professor Fiodorof, fully realising the importance of what he was going to say, answered:

" Science teaches us, sire, that it is an incurable disease. Yet those who are afflicted with it sometimes reach an advanced old age. Still, Alexis Nicolaïevitch is at the mercy of an accident."

The Czar hung his head and sadly murmured :

" That's just what the Czarina told me.   Well, if that is the case and Alexis can never serve his country as I should like him to, we have the right to keep him ourselves."

His mind was made up, and when the representatives of the Provisional Government and the Duma arrived from Petrograd that evening he handed them the Act of Abdication he had drawn up beforehand and in which he renounced for himself and his son the throne of Russia in favour of his brother, the Grand-Duke Michael Alexandrovitch.

I give a translation of this document which, by its nobility and the burning patriotism in every line, compelled the admiration of even the Czar's enemies :

THE ACT OF ABDICATION OF THE CZAR NICHOLAS II.

By the grace of God, We, Nicholas II., Emperor of all the Russias, Tsar of Poland, Grand-Duke of Finland, etc., etc. . . . to all Our faithful subjects make known :

In these days of terrible struggle against the external enemy who has been trying for three years to impose his will upon Our Fatherland, God has willed that Russia should be faced with a new and formidable trial. Troubles at home threaten to have a fatal effect on the ultimate course of this hard-fought war.   The destinies of Russia, the honour of Our heroic army, the welfare of the people and the whole future of Our dear country demand that the war should be carried to a victorious conclusion at any price.

Our cruel foe is making his supreme effort, and the moment is at hand in which Our valiant army, in concert with Our glorious allies, will overthrow him once and for all.

In these days, which are decisive for the existence of Russia, We think We should follow the voice of Our conscience by facilitating the closest co-operation of Our people and the organisation of all its resources for the speedy realisation of victory.

For these reasons, in accord with the Duma of the Empire, We think it Our duty to abdicate the Crown and lay down the supreme power.

Not desiring to be separated from Our beloved son, We bequeath Our heritage to Our brother, the Grand-Duke Michael Alexandrovitch, and give him Our blessing. We abjure him to govern in perfect accord with the representatives of the nation sitting in the legislative institutions, and to take a sacred oath in the name of the beloved Fatherland.

We appeal to all the loyal sons of the country, imploring them to fulfil their patriotic and holy duty of obeying their Czar in this sad time of national trial. We ask them to help him and the representatives of the nation to guide the Russian state into the path of prosperity and glory.

God help Russia.

The Czar had fallen. Germany was on the point of winning her greatest victory, but the fruits might still escape her. They would have escaped her if the intelligent section of the nation had recovered itself in time and had gathered round the Grand-Duke Michael, who, by his brother's desire—the Act of Abdication said so in terms—was to be a constitutional sovereign

in the full sense of the word.   Nothing prevented so desirable
a consummation, for Russia was not yet in the presence of one
of those great popular movements which defy all logic and
hurl nations into the gulf of the unknown.   The revolution
had been exclusively the work of the Petrograd population,
the majority of which would not have hesitated to rally
round the new ruler if the Provisional Government and the
Duma had set the example.   The army, which was still a well-
disciplined body, represented a serious force.   As for the great
bulk of the nation, it had not the slightest idea that anything
had passed.

This last chance of averting the catastrophe was lost
through thirst for power and fear of the Extremists.   The day
after the Czar's abdication the Grand-Duke Michael, acting on
the advice of all save two of the members of the Provisional
Government, renounced the throne in turn and resigned to a
constituent assembly the task of deciding what the future form
of government should be.

The irreparable step had been taken.   The removal of the
Czar had left in the minds of the masses a gaping void it was
impossible for them to fill.   They were left to their own
devices—a rudderless ship at the mercy of the waves—and
searching for an ideal, some article of faith which might replace
what they had lost, they found nothing but chaos around
them.

To finish her work of destruction, Germany had only to give
Lenin and his disciples a plentiful supply of money and let
them loose on Russia.   Lenin and his friends never dreamed of
talking to the peasants about a democratic republic or a
constituent assembly.   They knew it would have been waste
of breath.   As up-to-date prophets, they came to preach the

holy war and to try and draw these untutored millions by the attraction of a creed in which the finest teaching of Christ goes hand in hand with the worst sophisms—a creed which, thanks to the Jews, the adventurers of Bolshevism, was to be translated into the subjection of the *moujik* and the ruin of the country.

CHAPTER XVI
THE CZAR NICHOLAS II.

CHAPTER XVI

THE CZAR NICHOLAS II.

NICHOLAS II., desiring to say farewell to his troops, left Pskoff on March 16th and returned to G.H.Q. He stayed there until the 21st, living in the Governor's house as before and receiving General Alexeieff's report every day. The Dowager Empress, Marie Feodorovna, had come from Kieff to join the Czar, and she remained with him until the day he left for Tsarskoïe-Selo.

On the 21st the Commissioners sent by the Provisional Government and the Duma arrived at Mohileff. They instructed General Alexeieff to tell the Czar that on the orders of the Provisional Government he was under arrest, and that their duty was to conduct him to Tsarskoïe-Selo. The Commissioners' carriage was attached to the Czar's train and they all left together the same evening.

Before leaving G.H.Q. Nicholas II. insisted on taking leave of his troops by addressing to them the following Order of the Day :

PRIKAZE OF THE CHIEF OF STAFF TO THE COMMANDER-IN-CHIEF.

8 (21) March, 1917. No. 371.

I address my soldiers, who are dear to my heart, for the last time. Since I have renounced the Throne of Russia for myself and my son, power has been taken over by the Provisional Government which has been formed on the initiative of the Duma of the Empire.

May God help it to lead Russia into the path of glory and prosperity! May God help you, my glorious soldiers, to defend our Fatherland against a cruel enemy! For two and a half years you have endured the strain of hard service; much blood has been shed, great efforts have been made, and now the hour is at hand in which Russia and her glorious Allies will break the enemy's last resistance in one common, mightier effort.

This unprecedented war must be carried through to final victory. Anyone who thinks of peace or desires it at this moment is a traitor to his country and would deliver her over to the foe. I know that every soldier worthy of the name thinks as I do.

Do your duty, protect our dear and glorious country, submit to the Provisional Government, obey your leaders, and remember that any failure in duty can only profit the enemy.

I am firmly convinced that the boundless love you bear our great country is not dead within you. God bless you, and may St. George, the great martyr, lead you to victory!

NICHOLAS.

The Chief of the General Staff, ALEXEIEFF.

In this sad and tragic hour the Czar had only one desire—to make the task of the Government which had dethroned him easier. His only fear was that the events which had happened might have an evil effect on the army which the enemy could turn to his own advantage.

On the orders of the Minister of War this Order of the Day was never brought to the knowledge of the troops !

Why did Fate decree that the Czar Nicholas II. should reign at the beginning of the twentieth century and in one of the most troublous periods of history ? Endowed with remarkable personal qualities, he was the incarnation of all that was noblest and most chivalrous in the Russian nature. But he was weak. The soul of loyalty, he was the slave of his pledged word. His fidelity to the Allies, which was probably the cause of his death, proves it beyond doubt. He despised the methods of diplomacy and he was not a fighter. He was crushed down by events.

Nicholas II. was modest and timid ; he had not enough self-confidence : hence all his misfortunes. His first impulse was usually right. The pity was that he seldom acted on it because he could not trust himself. He sought the counsel of those he thought more competent than himself ; from that moment he could no longer master the problems that faced him. They escaped him. He hesitated between conflicting causes and often ended by following that to which he was personally least sympathetic.

The Czarina knew the Czar's irresolute character. As I have said, she considered she had a sacred duty to help him in his heavy task. Her influence on the Czar was very great and almost always unfortunate ; she made politics a matter of sentiment and personalities, and too often allowed herself to be swayed by her sympathies or antipathies, or by those of her *entourage.* Impulsive by nature, the Czarina was liable to emotional outbursts which made her give her confidence unreservedly to those she believed sincerely devoted to the country and the dynasty. Protopopoff was a case in point.

The Czar was always anxious to be just and to do the right thing. If he sometimes failed, the fault lies at the door of those who did their utmost to hide the truth from him and isolate him from his people. All his generous impulses were broken against the passive resistance of an omnipotent bureaucracy or were wilfully frustrated by those to whom he entrusted their realisation. He thought that personal initiative, however powerful and well meant, was nothing compared to those higher forces which direct the course of events. Hence that sort of mystical resignation in him which made him follow life rather than try to lead it. It is one of the characteristics of the Russian nature.

An essentially reflective man, he would have been perfectly happy to live as a private individual, but he was resigned to his lot, and humbly accepted the superhuman task which God had given him. He loved his people and his country with all the force of his nature ; he had a personal affection for the least of his subjects, those *moujiks* whose lot he earnestly desired to better.

What a tragic fate was that of this sovereign whose only desire during his reign was to be close to his people and who never succeeded in realising his wish. The fact is that he was well guarded, and by those whose interest it was that he should not succeed.[1]

---

[1] It was a great misfortune for the Czar Nicholas II. and the Czarina Alexandra Feodorovna that they ascended the throne so young. Like Louis XVI. and Marie Antoinette, they could have said, " Guard us, protect us, O God ! We are reigning too young ! "

History will ultimately give them their due. What was not written about Louis XVI. at the time of the French Revolution ? What accusations were levelled against him ? Was there any calumny of which he was not the victim ? Yet the children in France learn to-day that " he was honest and kind, and desired to do good " (Malet, *Révolution et Empire*, p. 312). It will be the same with Nicholas II., with the difference that he was a victim to his devotion to his country because he rejected all compromise with the enemy.

CHAPTER XVII

THE REVOLUTION SEEN FROM THE ALEXANDER PALACE—THE CZAR'S RETURN TO TSARSKOÏE-SELO

CHAPTER XVII

THE REVOLUTION SEEN FROM THE ALEX-ANDER PALACE—THE CZAR'S RETURN TO TSARSKOÏE-SELO

WHILE the dramatic events I have described in the preceding chapters were in progress at Pskoff and Mohileff the Czarina and her children, who had remained behind at the Alexander Palace, were passing through days of the most poignant anguish.

As we have seen, it was only after long hesitation that the Czar, in his anxiety, had decided on March 8th, 1917, to leave Tsarskoïe-Selo and go to G.H.Q.

His departure was a great blow to the Czarina, for to the fears aroused in her breast by the political situation had been added her anxiety about Alexis Nicolaïevitch. The Czarevitch had been in bed with measles for several days, and his condition had been aggravated by various complications. To crown everything, three of the Grand-Duchesses had also been taken ill, and there was no one but Marie Nicolaïevna to help the mother.

On March 10th we learned that trouble had broken out in Petrograd and that bloody collisions had taken place between police and demonstrators.

The fact was that for several days the shortage of food had produced feelings of bitter discontent in the poorer quarters of the city. There had been processions, and mobs had appeared in the streets demanding bread.

I realised that Her Majesty had a good deal on her mind, for, contrary to her usual habit, she spoke freely about political events, and told me that Protopopoff had accused the Socialists of conducting an active propaganda among railway employees with a view to preventing the provisioning of the city, and thus precipitating a revolution.

On the 11th the situation suddenly became very critical and the most alarming news arrived without warning. The mob made its way into the centre of the town, and the troops, who had been called in the previous evening, were offering but slight resistance.

I heard also that an Imperial *ukase* had ordered the sittings of the Duma to be suspended, but that, in view of the grave events in progress, the Assembly had disregarded the decree for its prorogation and decided to form an executive committee charged with the duty of restoring order.

The fighting was renewed with greater violence the next morning, and the insurgents managed to secure possession of the arsenal. Towards the evening I was told on the telephone from Petrograd that reserve elements of several regiments of the Guard—*e.g.*, the Paul, Preobrajensky, and other regiments —had made common cause with them. This piece of news absolutely appalled the Czarina. She had been extremely anxious since the previous evening, and realised that the peril was imminent.

She had spent these two days between the rooms of the Grand-Duchesses and that of Alexis Nicolaïevitch, who had taken a turn for the worse, but she always did her utmost to conceal her torturing anxiety from the invalids.

At half-past ten on the morning of the 13th the Czarina beckoned me to step into an adjoining room just as I was entering the Czarevitch's bedroom. She told me that the capital was actually in the hands of the revolutionaries and that the Duma had just set up a Provisional Government with Rodzianko at its head.

" The Duma has shown itself equal to the occasion," she said. " I think it has realised the danger which is threatening the country, but I'm afraid it is too late. A Revolutionary-Socialist Committee has been formed which will not recognise the authority of the Provisional Government. I have just received a telegram from the Czar saying he will be here at six in the morning, but he wants us to leave Tsarskoïe-Selo for Gatchina,[1] or else go to meet him. Please make all arrangements for Alexis's departure."

The necessary orders were given. Her Majesty was a prey to terrible doubt and hesitation. She informed Rodzianko of the serious condition of the Czarevitch and the Grand-Duchesses, but he replied : " When a house is burning the invalids are the first to be taken out."

At four o'clock Dr. Derevenko came back from the hospital and told us that the whole network of railways round Petrograd was already in the hands of the revolutionaries, so that we could not leave, and it was highly improbable that the Czar would be able to reach us.

About nine in the evening Baroness Buxhœveden entered my room. She had just heard that the garrison of Tsarskoïe-Selo had mutinied and that there was firing in the streets. She was going to tell the Czarina, who was with the Grand-Duchesses. As a matter of fact, she came into the corridor at

---

[1] Another Imperial residence, twelve miles south-west of Petrograd.

that moment and the Baroness told her how things stood. We went to the windows. We saw General Reissine, who had taken up position outside the palace at the head of two companies of the composite regiment. I also saw some marines of the bodyguard and cossacks of the escort. The park gates had been occupied in special strength, the men being drawn up in four ranks, ready to fire.

At that moment we heard on the telephone that the rebels were coming in our direction and had just killed a sentry less than five hundred yards from the palace. The sound of firing came steadily nearer and a fight seemed inevitable. The Czarina was horrorstruck at the idea that blood might be shed under her very eyes; she went out with Marie Nicolaïevna and exhorted the men to keep cool. She begged them to parley with the rebels. It was a terrible moment, and our hearts almost stopped beating with suspense. A single mistake and there would have been a hand-to-hand fight followed by bloodshed. However, the officers stepped in and a parley began. The rebels were impressed by the words of their old leaders and the resolute attitude of the troops which remained faithful.

The excitement gradually subsided and a neutral zone was fixed between the two camps.

Thus was the night passed, and in the morning formal orders from the Provisional Government arrived which put an end to the dreadful situation.

In the afternoon Her Majesty sent for the Grand Duke Paul and asked him if he knew where the Czar was. The Grand Duke did not know. When the Czarina questioned him about the situation he replied that in his opinion the grant of a constitution at once could alone avert the peril. The Czarina shared that view, but could do nothing, as she had been

IN THE CHAIR, THE GRAND-DUCHESS MARIE RECOVERING FROM HER
ILLNESS. ON THE LEFT, ANASTASIE NICOLAÏEVNA. ON THE RIGHT,
TATIANA NICOLAÏEVNA. APRIL, 1917.

THE FOUR GRAND-DUCHESSES IN THE PARK AT TSARSKOÏE-SELO.
MAY, 1917.

[Facing page 212.

unable to communicate with the Czar since the previous evening.

The day of the 15th passed in an oppressive suspense. At 3.30 a.m. next morning Dr. Botkin was called to the telephone by a member of the Provisional Government, who asked him for news of Alexis Nicolaïevitch. (We heard subsequently that a report of his death had been circulating in the city.)

The Czarina's ordeal was continued the next day. It was three days since she had had any news of the Czar and her forced inaction made her anguish all the more poignant.[1]

Towards the end of the afternoon the news of the Czar's abdication reached the palace. The Czarina refused to believe it, asserting it was a *canard*. But soon afterwards the Grand Duke Paul arrived to confirm it. She still refused to believe it, and it was only after hearing all the details he gave her that Her Majesty yielded to the evidence. The Czar had abdicated at Pskoff the previous evening in favour of his brother, the Grand Duke Michael.

The Czarina's despair almost defied imagination, but her great courage did not desert her. I saw her in Alexis Nicolaïe-vitch's room that same evening. Her face was terrible to see, but, with a strength of will which was almost superhuman, she had forced herself to come to the children's rooms as usual so that the young invalids, who knew nothing of what had happened since the Czar had left for G.H.Q., should suspect nothing.

Late at night we heard that the Grand Duke Michael had

---

[1] No one can have any idea of what the Czarina suffered during these days when she was despairing at her son's bedside and had no news of the Czar. She reached the extreme limits of human resistance in this last trial, in which originated that wonderful and radiant serenity which was to sustain her and her family to the day of their death.

renounced the throne, and that the fate of Russia was to be settled by the Constituent Assembly.

Next morning I found the Czarina in Alexis Nicolaïevitch's room. She was calm, but very pale. She looked very much thinner and ever so much older in the last few days.

In the afternoon Her Majesty received a telegram from the Czar in which he tried to calm her fears, and told her that he was at Mohileff pending the imminent arrival of the Dowager Empress.

Three days passed. At half-past ten on the morning of the 21st Her Majesty summoned me and told me that General Korniloff had been sent by the Provisional Government to inform her that the Czar and herself were under arrest and that all those who did not wish to be kept in close confinement must leave the palace before four o'clock. I replied that I had decided to stay with them.

" The Czar is coming back to-morrow. Alexis must be told everything. Will you do it ? I am going to tell the girls myself."

It was easy to see how she suffered when she thought of the grief of the Grand-Duchesses on hearing that their father had abdicated. They were ill, and the news might make them worse.

I went to Alexis Nicolaïevitch and told him that the Czar would be returning from Mohileff next morning and would never go back there again.

" Why ? "

" Your father does not want to be Commander-in-Chief any more."

He was greatly moved at this, as he was very fond of going to G.H.Q.

After a moment or two I added :

" You know your father does not want to be Czar any more, Alexis Nicolaïevitch."

He looked at me in astonishment, trying to read in my face what had happened.

" What ! Why ? "

" He is very tired and has had a lot of trouble lately."

" Oh yes ! Mother told me they stopped his train when he wanted to come here. But won't papa be Czar again after-wards ? "

I then told him that the Czar had abdicated in favour of the Grand Duke Michael, who had also renounced the throne.

" But who's going to be Czar, then ? "

" I don't know. Perhaps nobody now. . . ."

Not a word about himself. Not a single allusion to his rights as the Heir. He was very red and agitated.

There was a silence, and then he said :

" But if there isn't a Czar, who's going to govern Russia ? "

I explained that a Provisional Government had been formed and that it would govern the state until the Constituent Assembly met, when his uncle Michael would perhaps mount the throne.

Once again I was struck by the modesty of the boy.

At four o'clock the doors of the palace were closed. We were prisoners ! The composite regiment had been relieved by a regiment from the garrison of Tsarkoïe-Selo, and the soldiers on sentry duty were there not to protect us, but to keep guard over us.

At eleven o'clock on the morning of the 22nd the Czar arrived, accompanied by Prince Dolgorouky, the Marshal of the Court.   He went straight up to the children's room, where the Czarina was waiting for him.

After luncheon he went into the room of Alexis Nicolaïevitch, where I was, and greeted me with his usual unaffected kindness.   But I could tell by his pale, worn face that he too had suffered terribly during his absence.

Yet, despite the circumstances, the Czar's return was a day of rejoicing to his family.   The Czarina and Marie Nicolaïevna, as well as the other children, when they had been told what had occurred, had been a prey to such dreadful doubts and fears on his account !   It was a great comfort to be all together in such times of trial.   It seemed as if it made their troubles less unbearable, and as if their boundless love for each other was a dynamic force which enabled them to face any degree of suffering.

In spite of the self-control which was habitual with the Czar, he was unable to conceal his immense distress, though his soon recovered in the bosom of his family.   He spent most of the day with them, and otherwise read or went for walks with Prince Dolgorouky.   At first he had been forbidden to go into the park, and was only allowed the enjoyment of a small garden contiguous to the palace.   It was still under snow. A cordon of sentries was posted round it.

Yet the Czar accepted all these restraints with extraordinary serenity and moral grandeur.   No word of reproach ever passed his lips.   The fact was that his whole being was dominated by one passion, which was more powerful even than the bonds between himself and his family—love of country: We felt he was ready to forgive anything to those who were inflicting such humiliations upon him so long as they were capable of saving Russia.

THE CZARINA'S ROOM IN THE ALEXANDER PALACE. ON THE WALL, "MARIE ANTOINETTE AND HER CHILDREN," A TAPESTRY AFTER MADAME VIGEE-LEBRUN'S PICTURE PRESENTED BY THE FRENCH GOVERNMENT.

THE PORTRAIT GALLERY.

[Facing page 216.

The Czarina spent almost all her time on a *chaise longue* in the Grand-Duchesses' room, or else with Alexis Nicolaïevitch. Her anxieties and the emotional strain had exhausted her physically, but since the Czar's return she had found great moral relief, and lived closely with her own thoughts, speaking little and finally yielding to that urgent need for rest which had long assailed her. She was glad she need struggle no longer and that she could wholly devote herself to those she loved so tenderly.

She was now anxious about Marie Nicolaïevna only. The latter had been taken ill much later than her sisters, and her condition was aggravated by a severe attack of pneumonia of a virulent kind. Her constitution was excellent, but she had all she could do to survive. She was also the victim of her own devotion. This girl of seventeen had spent herself without reflection during the revolution. She had been her mother's greatest comfort and stand-by. During the night of March 13th she had been rash enough to go out with her mother to speak to the soldiers, thus exposing herself to the cold, even though she realised that her illness was beginning. Fortunately the other children were better, and already on the road to convalescence.

Our captivity at Tsarskoïe-Selo did not seem likely to last long, and there was talk about our imminent transfer to England. Yet the days passed and our departure was always being postponed. The fact was that the Provisional Government was obliged to deal with the advanced wing and gradually felt that its authority was slipping away from it. Yet we were only a few hours by railway from the Finnish frontier, and the necessity of passing through Petrograd was the only serious obstacle.

It would thus appear that if the authorities had acted resolutely and secretly it would not have been difficult to get the Imperial family to one of the Finnish ports and thus to some foreign country.   But they were afraid of responsibilities, and no one dare compromise himself.   Once more Fate was on guard !

CHAPTER XVIII

FIVE MONTHS' CAPTIVITY AT TSARSKOÏE-SELO
(MARCH—AUGUST, 1917)

CHAPTER XVIII

FIVE MONTHS' CAPTIVITY AT TSARSKOÏE-SELO

(MARCH—AUGUST, 1917)

THE Imperial family remained at Tsarskoïe-Selo until the
month of August, 1917. During the five months of this
internment with them I kept a diary of our life together. It
will be understood that delicacy of feeling prevents me from
reproducing it in its entirety. I wish to avoid as much as
possible bringing in people who are still alive. I shall, however, break through this reserve when it is a question of dealing
with incidents which throw light on the character of the Czar
and his family or their feelings during these long months of
trial.

Sunday, April 1st.—Alexis Nicolaïevitch feeling
much better. We went to church this morning, where we
found Their Majesties, the Grand-Duchesses Olga and
Tatiana, and the various members of the suite who are
sharing our captivity. When the priest prayed for the
success of the Russian and Allied armies the Czar and
Czarina knelt down, the whole congregation following
their example.

A few days ago, as I was leaving Alexis Nicolaïevitch's
room, I met ten soldiers wandering about in the passage.
I went up to them and asked what they wanted.

" We want to see the Heir "

" He's in bed and can't be seen."

" And the others ? "

" They are also unwell."

" And where is the Czar ? "

" I don't know."

" Will he be going out ? "

" I don't know ; but come, don't hang about here. There must be no noise because of the invalids ! "

They went back, walking on their toes and talking in low voices.   These are the soldiers depicted to us as wild revolutionaries hating their ex-Czar.

Tuesday, April 3rd.—To-day Kerenski came to the palace for the first time.   He went through all the rooms and noted all the sentry-posts, wishing to assure himself in person that we are well guarded.   Before leaving he had a fairly long conversation with the Czar and Czarina.

Wednesday, April 4th.—Alexis Nicolaïevitch related to me yesterday's conversation between Kerensky and the Czar and Czarina.

The whole family was collected in the apartment of the Grand-Duchesses.   Kerensky entered and introduced himself, saying :

" I am the Procurator-General, Kerensky."

Then he shook hands all round.   Turning to the Czarina, he said :

" The Queen of England asks for news of the ex-Czarina."

Her Majesty blushed violently.   It was the first time that she had been addressed as ex-Czarina.   She

THE CZAR, HIS CHILDREN AND THEIR COMPANIONS IN CAPTIVITY CONVERT-
ING THE LAWNS OF THE PARK INTO A KITCHEN-GARDEN. MAY, 1917.

Near to the wooden hut, the Czarina in white, with a parasol, and two of the Grand-Duchesses.
In the centre, to the right, the Czar Nicholas II. The Alexander Palace in the background.

[Facing page 222.

answered that she was fairly well, but that her heart was troubling her as usual. Kerensky went on :

" Anything I begin I always carry through to the bitter end, with all my might. I wanted to see everything myself, to verify everything so as to be able to report at Petrograd, and it will be better for you."

He then asked the Czar to go with him into the next room as he wished to speak to him in private. He went in first and the Czar followed.

After his departure, the Czar told us that no sooner were they alone than Kerensky said to him :

" You know I've succeeded in getting the death penalty abolished ? . . . I've done this in spite of the fact that a great number of my comrades have died, martyrs to their convictions."

Was he trying to make a display of his magnanimity, and insinuating that he was saving the Czar's life though the latter had done nothing to deserve it ?

He then spoke of our departure, which he still hopes to be able to arrange. When ? Where ? How ? He did not know himself, and asked that the matter should not be discussed.

This has been a hard blow for Alexis Nicolaïevitch. He has not yet realised their new situation. It was the first time he had seen his father receive orders and obey like a subordinate.

It is worthy of note that Kerensky arrived at the palace in one of the Czar's private cars, driven by a chauffeur from the Imperial garage.

Friday, April 6th.—The Czar told me to-day of the distress the papers cause him. It is the ruin of the

army ; no more hierarchy or discipline. The officers
are afraid of their men and are spied upon by them.
One feels the Czar is hard hit by the collapse of the army
which is so dear to him.

Sunday, April 8th.—After Mass, Kerensky announced
to the Czar that he was obliged to separate him from
the Czarina—that he will have to live apart, only seeing
Her Majesty at meals, and that on condition that only
Russian is spoken. Tea, too, may be taken together,
but in the presence of an officer, as no servants are
present.

A little later the Czarina came up to me in a great
state of agitation, and said :

" To think of his acting like this to the Czar, playing
this low trick after his self-sacrifice and his abdication
to avoid civil war ; how mean, how despicable ! The
Czar would not have had a single Russian shed his blood
for him. He has always been ready to renounce all
when he knew that it was for the good of Russia."

A moment later she went on :

" Yes, this horrible bitterness must be endured too."

Monday, April 9th.—I learn that Kerensky had
intended at first to isolate the Czarina, but it was
pointed out to him that it would be inhuman to separate
a mother from her sick children ; it was then that he
decided to isolate the Czar.

April 13th, Good Friday.—In the evening the whole
family went to Confession.

Saturday, April 14th.—In the morning, at half-past
nine, Mass and Holy Communion. In the evening, at
half-past eleven, everyone went to church for the

midnight service. Colonel Korovitchenko, the Commandant of the palace and friend of Kerensky, and the three officers of the guard were also present. The service lasted until two o'clock, when we went to the library to exchange the traditional greetings. The Czar, according to Russian custom, embraced all the men present, including the Commandant and officers of the guard, who had remained with him. The two men could not hide their emotion at this spontaneous act.

We then took our places at a round table for the Easter meal. Their Majesties sat facing one another. There were seventeen of us, including the two officers. The Grand-Duchesses Olga and Marie were not present, nor Alexis Nicolaïevitch. The comparative animation which marked the beginning soon relapsed and conversation flagged. His Majesty was particularly silent. Was it sadness or fatigue ?

Sunday, April 15th, Easter Day.—We went out for the first time with Alexis Nicolaïevitch on the terrace in front of the palace. A superb spring day.

In the evening at seven o'clock a religious service upstairs in the children's apartments. There were only fifteen of us. I noticed that the Czar crossed himself piously when the priest prayed for the Provisional Government.

On the following day, as the weather was still very fine, we went out into the park, where we are now allowed to take the air, followed by officers of the guard and sentries.

Wishing to take a little physical exercise, we amused ourselves by clearing the sluices of the pond of the ice

P

which was blocking them. A crowd of soldiers and civilians soon lined up along the park railing and watched our work. After some time the officer of the guard went up to the Czar and told him that the Commandant of the Tsarskoïe-Selo garrison had just warned him that he feared a hostile demonstration or even an attempt on the lives of the Imperial family, and he would ask us not to remain where we were. The Czar answered that he had no fear, and that the good people were not annoying him in any way.

Wednesday, April 18th.—Whenever we go out, soldiers, with fixed bayonets and under the command of an officer, surround us and keep pace with us. We look like convicts with their warders. The instructions are changed daily, or perhaps the officers interpret them each in his own way !

This afternoon, when we were going back to the palace after our walk, the sentry on duty at the gate stopped the Czar, saying :

" You cannot pass, sir."

The officer with us here intervened. Alexis Nicolaïevitch blushed hotly to see the soldier stop his father.

Friday, April 20th.—We now go out regularly twice a day : in the morning from eleven till noon, in the afternoon from half-past two to five. We all collect in the semi-circular hall and wait for the officer commanding the guard to come and open the gates into the park. We go out ; the officer on duty and soldiers fall in behind us and take station round the place where we stop to work. The Czarina and Grand-Duchesses Olga and Marie are still confined to their rooms.

THE CZAR WORKING IN THE KITCHEN-GARDEN. BEHIND HIM THE
OFFICER ON DUTY. ON THE RIGHT THE SAILOR, NAGORNY. BEHIND,
COUNTESS HENDRIKOF.

THE CZARINA, IN AN INVALID CHAIR, WORKING AT SOME EMBROIDERY
AND WATCHING HER FAMILY GARDENING.

[Facing page 226.

Sunday, April 22nd.—We are forbidden to go to the pond ; we have to keep near the palace and not go outside the radius which has been fixed for us. In the distance we saw a crowd of several hundred people curious to see us.

Wednesday, April 25th.—Kerensky returned to the palace. Dr. Botkin has taken advantage of this to ask if it would be possible to transfer the Imperial family to Livadia on account of the children's health. Kerensky replied that it was quite impossible for the moment. He then went to see Their Majesties, and remained some time. Kerensky's attitude towards the Czar is no longer what it was at the beginning ; he has given up his judicial bearing. I am convinced that he is beginning to understand what the Czar is and yielding to his moral ascendancy like all who come near him. Kerensky has requested the papers to put an end to their campaign against the Czar, and more especially the Czarina. These calumnies simply pour oil on the flames. He feels his responsibility towards the captives. But not a word about our departure abroad. That proves his powerlessness.

Sunday, April 29th.—In the evening a long conversation with Their Majesties on the subject of Alexis Nicolaïevitch's lessons. We must find a way out since we have no longer any tutors. The Czar is going to make himself responsible for History and Geography, the Czarina will take charge of his religious instruction. The other subjects will be shared between Baroness Buxhœveden (English), Mlle. Schneider (Arithmetic) Dr. Botkin (Russian) and myself.

Monday, April 30th.—This morning the Czar greeted me with : " Good morning, dear colleague "—he has just given Alexis Nicolaïevitch his first lesson.   Always the same serenity, the same anxiety to be agreeable to those who share his captivity.   He is an example and an encouragement to us.

I have given Tatiana Nicolaïevna the article in the *Journal des Dèbats* of April 18th, 1917, signed A. G. (Auguste Gauvain) for her parents to read.

It is apparent that the régime to which we are being subjected is becoming continually more severe.

Tuesday, May 1st.—For the first time Russia celebrates May 1st.   We hear the bands and see the processions of demonstrators pass along the park railings.

This evening the Czar returned to me the copy of the *Journal des Dèbats* dealing with his abdication.   He told me it had given the Czarina pleasure to read this article, which tried to be fair to him.   Its tone was a contrast to that of the English papers.

Thursday, May 3rd.—The Czar told me this evening that the news has not been good for several days.   The Extremist parties demand that France and England should declare themselves ready to make peace " without annexations or indemnities."   Deserters are becoming more and more numerous and the army is melting away.   Will the Provisional Government be strong enough to continue the war ?

The Czar is following events with acute interest ; he is anxious, but still hopes that the country will pull itself together and remain faithful to the Allies.

Sunday, May 13th.—This is the second day we have

spent making a kitchen garden on one of the lawns of the park. We began by taking up the turf, carrying away the sod on barrows and arranging it in heaps. Everyone helped : the family, ourselves, and the servants, who for some time have been going out with us. Several soldiers of the guard even have come to help us !

The Czar has looked very preoccupied during the last few days. As we were coming back from our walk he said to me :

" It seems Rvssky has resigned. He had asked that an offensive should be undertaken. (One *asks* now ; one no longer gives orders !) The Soldiers' Committees refused. If this is true it is the end ! What humiliation ! To remain on the defensive and not attack is suicide ! We're going to let our allies be crushed, and then it will be our turn."

Monday, May 14th.—The Czar returned to our conversation of yesterday, adding :

" What gives me a little hope is our love of exaggeration. I can't believe that our army at the front is as bad as they say ; it can't have fallen to this extent in two months."

Thursday, May 17th.—It appears that the end has been reached of the serious Government crisis that has lasted a fortnight. The news from Petrograd seems less bad. The new Council of Ministers, reconstituted with the addition of a few representatives of the soldiers and workmen, will perhaps succeed in establishing its authority. Meanwhile anarchy is everywhere gaining ground.

Saturday, May 19th.—The Czar's birthday. (He is forty-nine.) Mass and congratulations.

Sunday, May 27th.—For some time we have been allowed only a very small supply of wood, and it is intensely cold everywhere. Mme. Narichkine (Grand-Mistress of the Court) has been taken ill, and was sent away to-day, the state of her health demanding care which cannot be given here. She was in despair at the idea of leaving us, for she knows she will not be permitted to return to the palace.

Saturday, June 2nd.—We are still working every day at the kitchen garden. We are watering it from a tub which we take turns to drag.

Sunday, June 10th.—A few days ago the children were playing on their island (an artificial islet in the middle of a little lake). Alexis Nicolaïevitch was practising handling his little gun, which he thinks a lot of, as it was given to the Czar when he was a boy by his father. An officer came up to us. He told me that the soldiers had decided to take the gun away from the Czarevitch, and were coming for it. When he heard this, Alexis Nicolaïevitch put down his toy and joined the Czarina, who was sitting on the grass a few yards from us. A moment later the officer on duty came with two soldiers and demanded that the " weapon " should be given up. I tried to intervene and make them understand that the gun was not a weapon but a toy. It was no use : they took possession of it. Alexis Nicolaïevitch began to sob. His mother asked me to make another attempt to convince the soldiers, but I did not succeed any better than the first time, and they went off with their prize.

Half an hour later the officer on duty took me aside

THE GRAND-DUCHESS TATIANA CARRIES TURF WITH THE HELP OF
ONE OF THE GUARDS.

THE CZAR AND HIS SERVANT JURAVSKY SAWING THE TRUNK OF A
TREE THEY HAD FELLED.

[*Facing page* 230.

and asked me to tell the Czarevitch that he was greatly distressed at what he had had to do. After trying in vain to dissuade the men, he had chosen to come with them to prevent any discourtesy on their part.

Colonel Kobylinsky [1] was annoyed to hear of the incident, and brought back the little gun to Alexis Nicolaïevitch piece by piece. Since then he has only played with it in his room.

Friday, June 15th.—We finished our kitchen garden some time ago and it is now in splendid condition. We have every imaginable kind of vegetable, and five hundred cabbages. The servants, too, have made a garden on their side of the palace, where they can cultivate what they like. We went to help them dig it —the Czar too.

To occupy our leisure now that we have finished our work on the garden, we have asked and obtained permission to cut down the dead trees in the park, so we go from place to place, followed by a guard which moves when we move. We are beginning to be quite skilful woodcutters. This will give us a supply of wood for next winter.

Friday, June 22nd.—As the Grand-Duchesses were losing all their hair as the result of their illness, their heads have been shaved. When they go out in the park they wear scarves arranged so as to conceal the fact. Just as I was going to take their photographs, at a sign from Olga Nicolaïevna they all suddenly removed their headdress. I protested, but they insisted, much amused

---

[1] Colonel Kobylinsky shortly before had replaced Colonel Korovitchenko as Commandant of the palace.

at the idea of seeing themselves photographed like this, and looking forward to seeing the indignant surprise of their parents. Their good spirits reappear from time to time in spite of everything. It is their exuberant youth.

Sunday, June 24th.—The days follow one another, all alike, divided between lessons and walks. This morning the Czar told me of a rather amusing incident which has broken the monotony of our seclusion.

He was reading aloud yesterday evening in the red hall to the Czarina and Grand-Duchesses. Suddenly, about eleven o'clock, a servant entered in a great state of agitation and announced that the Commandant requested an immediate interview with the Czar. The latter thought that something very serious must have happened at Petrograd—a great armed demonstration by the Bolsheviks against the Provisional Government was expected—and he gave orders for him to be shown in. The officer entered, accompanied by two non-commissioned officers. He explained that he had been summoned by a shot from a sentry, who, from the park, had noticed signals with red and green lights from the room in which the family were sitting. General amazement. What signals ? What did it all mean ? Great excitement on the part of the Czarina and Grand-Duchesses. The officer then gave orders for the curtains to be closely drawn—it was stiflingly hot—and was about to retire. At this moment one of the N.C.O.'s came forward and explained the mystery. The Grand-Duchess Anastasie Nicolaïevna was sitting on the window-ledge doing needlework. Each time she bent forward to pick up from the table the things she required for her work she was covering and uncovering in turn two lamps with green and red shades by which the Czar was reading. The officer retired in confusion.

Monday, July 2nd.—We have learned that an offensive has been launched in the direction of Tarnopol, and is being successfully developed.

Tuesday, July 3rd.—A *Te Deum* for the military successes which seem to presage a great victory. The Czar, radiant, brought Alexis Nicolaïevitch the evening paper and read him the *communiqués*.

Thursday, July 12th.—The news from the front is not good. The offensive which had begun so well is turning against the Russians.

Sunday, July 15th.—Nothing new in our captivity. The only distraction is going out. It is very hot, and for some days Alexis Nicolaïevitch has been bathing in the pond round the children's island. It is a great joy to him.

Wednesday, July 25th.—The check is becoming more and more serious, the retreat deeper. The Czar is greatly affected.

Thursday, August 9th.—I learn that the Provisional Government has decided on the transfer of the Imperial family. The destination is kept secret; we are all hoping it will be the Crimea.

Saturday, August 11th.—We have been told that we must provide ourselves with warm clothing. So we are not to be taken south. A great disappointment.

Sunday, August 12th. (July 30th O.S.).—Alexis Nicolaïevitch's birthday (he is thirteen). At the request of the Czarina, the miraculous ikon of the Holy

234 Thirteen Years at the Russian Court

Virgin has been brought from the church of Znamenia. Our departure is fixed for to-morrow. Colonel Kobylinsky has confided to me as a great secret that we are to be transferred to Tobolsk.

Monday, August 13*th.*—We were told to be ready by midnight; the train was ordered for one o'clock. Final preparations. Farewell visit to the children's island, kitchen garden, etc. Shortly before one in the morning everyone collected in the semi-circular hall, which was full of luggage. The Grand-Duke Michael arrived with Kerensky and had an interview with the Czar, who was delighted to see his brother again before his departure.

The train which was to take us had not yet arrived; there appears to have been some difficulty with the railway men in Petrograd, who suspected that city to be the destination of the Imperial family. The hours passed in waiting, which grew more and more trying. Should we be able to start ? It began to seem doubtful. (This incident showed up the powerlessness of the Government.) At last, about five o'clock, we were told that all was ready. We took leave of those of our fellow-captives who could not leave with us.[1] Our hearts were wrung at the thought of leaving Tsarskoïe-

---

[1] These were Count and Countess Benckendorf, whom their great age and uncertain state of health prevented from following us; Baroness Buxhœveden, who was kept back by illness and was to join us at Tobolsk as soon as she could, and a certain number of servants. Kerensky had asked the Czar whether he wished Count Benckendorf to be replaced. The Czar had replied that he would be very glad for General Tatichtchef to come and share his captivity. On learning his Czar's wish General Tatichtchef only allowed himself time to put his affairs in order, and a few hours later started, valise in hand, for Tsarskoïe-Selo. We found him in the train at the moment of departure. General Tatichtchef held no Court appointment; he was one of the Czar's numerous aides-de-camp.

THE GRAND-DUCHESSES TATIANA AND ANASTASIE TAKING A WATER-
BUTT TO THE KITCHEN-GARDEN. JUNE, 1917.

THE IMPERIAL FAMILY'S SUITE AT TSARSKOÏE-SELO IN THE SUMMER
OF 1917.

From left to right, behind Countess Benckendorff, seated : Prince Dolgorouky, the
author, Countess Hendrikof, Baroness de Buxhœveden, Mlle. Schneider, Count
Benckendorff, and Dr. Derevenko.

[Facing page 234.

Selo, to which we were bound by so many memories, and this departure for the unknown was marked by great sadness. Just as our cars were leaving the park we were surrounded by a detachment of cavalry, which escorted us as far as the little station of Alexandrovka. We took our places in the compartments, which are very comfortable. Half an hour passed and then the train slowly moved away. It was ten minutes to six.

CHAPTER XIX

OUR CAPTIVITY AT TOBOLSK
(AUGUST—DECEMBER, 1917)

CHAPTER XIX

OUR CAPTIVITY AT TOBOLSK
(AUGUST—DECEMBER, 1917)

WHAT reasons had the Council of Ministers for transporting the Imperial family to Tobolsk ?

It is difficult to say definitely. When Kerensky told the Czar of the proposed transfer he explained the necessity by saying that the Provisional Government had resolved to take energetic measures against the Bolsheviks ; this would result in a period of disturbance and armed conflict of which the Imperial family might be the first victims ; it was therefore his duty to put them out of danger. It has been claimed in other quarters that it was an act of weakness in face of the Extremists, who, uneasy at seeing in the army the beginnings of a movement in favour of the Czar, demanded his exile to Siberia. However this may be, the journey of the Imperial family from Tsarskoïe-Selo to Tobolsk was effected under comfortable conditions and without any noteworthy incidents.

Leaving on August 14th at 6 a.m., we reached Tioumen— the nearest railway station to Tobolsk—on the evening of the 17th, and a few hours later boarded the *Rouss*.

On the following day we passed the native village of Rasputin, and the family, gathered on the deck, were able to observe the house of the *staretz*, which stood out clearly from among the *isbas*. There was nothing to surprise them in this event, for Rasputin had foretold that it would be so, and chance once more seemed to confirm his prophetic words.

On the 19th, towards the end of the afternoon, we suddenly saw at a bend in the river the crenellated silhouette of the Kremlin, which dominates Tobolsk, and an hour later we reached our destination.

The house which was to receive us not being ready, we were forced to remain for some days on the boat which had brought us, and it was not until August 26th that we moved into our new quarters.

The family occupied the whole of the first floor of the Governor's house, a spacious and comfortable building. The suite lived in Korniloff's house, belonging to a rich merchant of Tobolsk, and situated on the other side of the road almost facing ours. The guard was formed by soldiers of the former rifle regiments of the Imperial family who had come with us from Tsarskoïe-Selo. They were under the orders of Colonel Kobylinsky, a generous man who had become sincerely attached to those in his charge ; he did all he could to ameliorate their lot.

At first the conditions of our captivity were very similar to those at Tsarkoïe-Selo. We had all that was necessary. The Czar and children nevertheless suffered from lack of space. Their exercise was confined to a very small kitchen garden and a yard which had been formed by enclosing with a fence a broad and little-frequented street running along the south-east side of the house in which they lived. It was very little, and they were exposed to the observation of the soldiers, whose barracks overlooked the whole of the space reserved for us. On the other hand, the members of the suite and servants were freer than at Tsarskoïe-Selo, at any rate to begin with, and

THE GRAND-DUCHESS TATIANA SITTING AT THE FURTHEST POINT
THE PRISONERS WERE ALLOWED TO GO IN THE PARK OF TSARSKOÏE-
SELO.

ALEXIS NICOLAÏEVITCH JOINS HIS SISTER, THE GRAND-DUCHESS
TATIANA.

[Facing page 240.

were allowed to go into the town or immediate surroundings

In September Commissary Pankratof arrived at Tobolsk, having been sent by Kerensky. He was accompanied by his deputy, Nikolsky—like himself, an old political exile. Pankratof was quite a well-informed man, of gentle character, the typical enlightened fanatic. He made a good impression on the Czar and subsequently became attached to the children. But Nikolsky was a low type, whose conduct was most brutal. Narrow and stubborn, he applied his whole mind to the daily invention of fresh annoyances. Immediately after his arrival he demanded of Colonel Kobylinsky that we should be forced to have our photographs taken. When the latter objected that this was superfluous, since all the soldiers knew us—they were the same as had guarded us at Tsarskoïe-Selo—he replied: " It was forced on us in the old days, now it's their turn." It had to be done, and henceforward we had to carry our identity cards with a photograph and identity number.

The religious services were at first held in the house, in the large hall on the first floor. The priest of the Church of the Annunciation, his deacon, and four nuns from the Yvanovsky Convent, were authorised to attend the services. As, however, there was no consecrated altar, it was impossible to celebrate Mass. This was a great privation for the family. Finally, on September 21st, the festival of the Nativity of the Virgin, the prisoners were allowed for the first time to go to the church. This pleased them greatly, but the consolation was only to be repeated very rarely. On these occasions we rose very early and, when everyone had collected in the yard, went out through a little gate leading on to the public garden, which we crossed between two lines of soldiers. We always attended the first Mass of the morning, and were almost alone in the

Q

church, which was dimly lighted by a few candles ; the public was rigorously excluded. While going and returning I have often seen people cross themselves or fall on their knees as Their Majesties passed. On the whole, the inhabitants of Tobolsk were still very attached to the Imperial family, and our guards had repeatedly to intervene to prevent them standing under the windows or removing their hats and crossing themselves as they passed the house.

Meanwhile our life gradually settled down along definite lines, and by mobilising all our resources we managed to resume the education of the Czarevitch and two youngest Grand-Duchesses. The lessons began at nine o'clock, and were broken off from eleven to twelve for a walk, which was always shared by the Czar. As there was no schoolroom, the lessons were given sometimes in the large hall on the first floor, sometimes in Alexis Nicolaïevitch's room or mine. I lived on the ground floor in what had been the Governor's study. At one o'clock we all assembled for lunch. The Czarina, when she was not well, often took her meals in her own apartments with Alexis Nicolaïevitch. About two o'clock we used to go out again and walk about or play until four.

The Czar was suffering a great deal from lack of physical exercise. Colonel Kobylinsky, to whom he complained of this, had beech-trunks brought and bought some saws and axes, and we were able to cut the wood we required for the kitchen and stoves. This was one of our great outdoor distractions during our captivity at Tobolsk, even the Grand-Duchesses becoming very keen on this new pastime.

After tea, lessons were resumed until about half-past six. Dinner was an hour later, after which we went up to the large hall for coffee. We had all been invited to spend the evening with the family, and this soon became a regular habit for several of us. Games were organised and ingenuity shown in finding amusements to break the monotony of our captivity. When it began to get very cold, and the large hall became impossible, we took refuge in the adjoining room, which was Their Majesties' drawing-room, the only really comfortable apartment in the house. The Czar would often read aloud while the Grand-Duchesses did needlework or played with us. The Czarina regularly played one or two games of bezique with General Tatichtchef and then took up her work or reclined in her armchair. In this atmosphere of family peace we passed the long winter evenings, lost in the immensity of distant Siberia.

One of the greatest privations during our captivity at Tobolsk was the almost complete absence of news. Letters only reached us very irregularly and after long delay. As for newspapers, we were reduced to a nasty local rag printed on packing paper, which only gave us telegrams several days old and generally distorted and cut down.

The Czar eagerly followed the development of events in Russia. He realised that the country was rushing towards ruin. He had a moment of fresh hope when General Kornilof offered Kerensky to march on Petrograd to put an end to the Bolshevik agitation, which was becoming more and more menacing. His disappointment was very great when the Provisional Government rejected this final chance of salvation. He saw in this the only means that remained perhaps of avoiding the imminent catastrophe. I then for the first time heard the Czar regret his abdication. He had made this decision in the hope that those who had wished to get rid of him would be capable of making a success of the war and saving Russia. He had feared that resistance on his part might give rise to a civil war in the presence of the enemy, and had been unwilling that the blood of a single Russian should be shed for him. But had not his departure been almost immediately followed by the appearance of Lenin and his acolytes, the paid agents of Germany, whose criminal propaganda had destroyed the army and corrupted the country ? It now gave him pain to see that his renunciation had been in vain, and that by his departure in the interests of his country he had in reality done her an ill turn. This idea was to haunt him more and more, and finally gave rise to grave moral anxiety.

About November 15th we learnt that the Provisional Government was overthrown and that the Bolsheviks had again come into power. But this event did not immediately react on our life, and it was not until some months later, as we shall see, that it occurred to them to turn their attention to us.

The weeks passed and the news which reached us grew worse and worse. It was, however, very difficult for us to follow events and grasp their purport, for the information at our disposal did not allow us to understand the causes or calculate the consequences ; we were, so far, so isolated from the entire world. And even if we succeeded in getting a rough knowledge of what was happening in Russia, the rest of Europe was almost a closed book.

Meanwhile the Bolshevik doctrines had begun their destructive work in the detachment which was guarding us and which hitherto had been fairly proof against them. It was composed of very varied elements : the men of the 1st and 4th Regiments were for the most part favourably disposed towards the Imperial family, and especially towards the children. The Grand-Duchesses, with that simplicity which was their charm, loved to talk to these men, who seemed to them to be linked with the past in the same way as themselves. They questioned them about their families, their villages, or the battles in which they had taken part in the great war. Alexis Nicolaïevitch, who to them was still " the Heir," had also won their hearts, and they took trouble to please him and find amusements for him. One section of the 4th Regiment, composed almost exclusively of the older classes, was particularly conspicuous in its attachment, and it was always a delight to the family to see these good fellows come back on duty. On these days the Czar and children used to go secretly to the guardhouse and converse or play draughts with the men, whose conduct was never in a single instance anything but strictly correct. Here they were once surprised by Commissary Pankratof, who stood astounded on the doorstep, looking through his spectacles at this unexpected sight. The Czar, seeing his disconcerted appearance, motioned to him to come and sit at the table. But the Commissary evidently thought he was out of place ; muttering a few unintelligible words, he turned on his heel and fled, discomfited.

Pankratof, as I have said, was a fanatic imbued with humanitarian principles ; he was not a bad fellow. Immediately after his arrival he had organised classes for the soldiers to initiate them in Liberal doctrines, and did all he could to develop their patriotism and citizenship. But his efforts recoiled upon himself. A convinced adversary of the Bolsheviks, he was in reality merely preparing the ground for them and, without realising it, helping towards the success of their ideas. As will be seen, he was destined to be the first victim.

The men of the 2nd Regiment had from the outset been

distinguished by revolutionary sentiments ; at Tsarskoïe-Selo they had already been the cause of a good deal of annoyance to their prisoners. The Bolshevik *coup d'état* increased their authority and audacity ; they had managed to form a " Soldiers' Committee," which tended further to restrict our régime and gradually to substitute its authority for that of Colonel Kobylinsky. We had proof of its ill-will on the occasion of Baroness Buxhœveden's arrival (the end of December O.S.). She had shared our captivity at Tsarskoïe-Selo, and it was only the state of her health that had prevented her from leaving with us. She had no sooner recovered than she came, with Kerensky's permission, to rejoin the Czarina. The Soldiers' Committee flatly refused to let her enter the house, and she had to find accommodation in the town. This was a great grief to the Czarina and the whole family, who had been looking forward very impatiently to her arrival.

Thus we reached Christmas.

The Czarina and Grand-Duchesses had for many weeks been preparing with their own hands a present for each of us and each of the servants. Her Majesty distributed some woollen waistcoats which she had knitted herself. With such touching thoughtfulness as this she tried to show her gratitude to those who had remained faithful.

On December 24th the priest came to the house for Vespers ; everyone then assembled in the large hall, and the children were full of delight at the " surprise " prepared for us. We now felt part of one large family ; we did our best to forget the preoccupations and distresses of the time in order to enjoy to the full and in complete unity these moments of peaceful intimacy.

The next day, Christmas Day, we went to church. By the

IN CAPTIVITY AT TOBOLSK

AT TOBOLSK, WHERE THEY WERE INTERNED FROM SEPTEMBER, 1917, TO APRIL, 1918. THE CZAR AND HIS CHILDREN ENJOY THE SIBERIAN SUNSHINE ON THE ROOF OF A GREENHOUSE.

From left to right : The Grand-Duchesses Olga and Anastasie, the Czar and the Czarevitch, the Grand-Duchess Tatiana, the Grand-Duchess Marie (standing). The Czarina was confined to her room, indisposed.

Facing page 246

orders of the priest the deacon intoned the *Mnogoletié* (the prayer for the long life of the Imperial family). This was an imprudence which was bound to bring reprisals. The soldiers, with threats of death, demanded that the prayer should be revoked. This incident marred the pleasant memories which this day should have left in our minds. It also brought us fresh annoyances and the supervision became still stricter.

CHAPTER XX

END OF OUR CAPTIVITY AT TOBOLSK
(JANUARY—MAY, 1918)

CHAPTER XX

END OF OUR CAPTIVITY AT TOBOLSK
(JANUARY—MAY, 1918)

ON January 1st/14th, 1914, I resumed the diary I had given up when we were transferred to Tobolsk. I shall give a few extracts from it as I did when describing our captivity at Tsarskoïe-Selo.

Monday, January 14th (January 1st O.S.).—This morning we went to church, where the new priest officiated for the first time. Father Vassilief (the cause of the incident mentioned in the preceding chapter) has been transferred by Archbishop Hermogenes to the monastery of Abalatsky.

Tuesday, January 15th.—At 2 p.m. there was a meeting of the committee of our garrison. It was decided by 100 votes to 85 to prohibit the wearing of epaulettes by officers and men.

Thursday, January 17th.—Colonel Kobylinsky came this morning. He wore mufti rather than wear his uniform without epaulettes.

Friday, January 18th.—The priest and choir [1] arrived at 3 o'clock. To-day is the Blessing of the Waters and the first time the new priest has officiated in

---

[1] The four nuns who used to come to sing at first had been replaced by the choir of one of the Tobolsk churches.

the house.   When it was Alexis Nicolaïevitch's turn to kiss the cross held out by the priest the latter bent down and kissed his forehead.   After dinner General Tatichtchef and Prince Dolgorouky came to beg the Czar to remove his epaulettes in order to avoid a hostile demonstration by the soldiers.   At first it seemed as though the Czar would refuse, but, after exchanging a look and a few words with the Czarina, he recovered his self-control and yielded for the sake of his family.

Saturday, January 19*th.*—We went to church this morning.   The Czar was wearing a Caucasian cloak, which is always worn without epaulettes.   Alexis Nicolaïevitch had hidden his under his " bachelik " (a sort of Caucasian muffler).   To-day the Czarina, on behalf of the Czar and herself, invited me to take evening tea [1] with them in future, when I don't feel too tired after my lessons.   I did not withdraw therefore at 10 o'clock when the Grand-Duchesses retired.   (Alexis Nicolaïevitch always goes to bed at nine o'clock.)

Monday, January 21*st.*—A heavy fall of snow last night.   We began to build a " snow mountain."

Friday, January 25*th* (January 12th O.S.).—Tatiana Nicolaïevna's birthday.   *Te Deum* in the house.   Fine winter's day; sunshine; 15° Réaumur.   Went on building the snow mountain as usual.   The soldiers of the guard came to help us.

Wednesday, January 30*th.*—To-day the friendly section of the 4th Regiment was on duty.   The Czar

---

[1] For this tea, which the Czarina poured out herself, Their Majesties were attended by Countess Hendrikof, lady-in-waiting, General Tatichtchef, Prince Dolgorouky, and, when their duties permitted, Mlle. Schneider and Doctor Botkin.   I am now the sole survivor of these evening tea-parties at Tobolsk.

THE GOVERNOR'S HOUSE AT TOBOLSK WHERE THE IMPERIAL FAMILY WERE INTERNED.

The Grand-Duchesses Marie and Anastasie on the balcony.

Barracks of the detachment which guarded the Czar.
The guard being changed.

[*Facing page* 252.

and children spent several hours with the soldiers in the guard-house.

Saturday, February 2nd.—23° R. below zero. Prince Dolgorouky and I watered the snow mountain. We carried thirty buckets of water. It was so cold that the water froze on the way from the kitchen tap to the mountain. Our buckets and the snow mountain " steamed." To-morrow the children can begin tobogganing.

Monday, February 4th.—The thermometer is said to have dropped last night below 30° Réaumur (37° Centigrade). Terrible wind. The Grand-Duchesses' bedroom is a real ice-house.

Wednesday, February 6th.—It appears that on the initiative of the 2nd Regiment the soldiers have decided that Commissary Pankratof and his deputy, Nikolsky, must resign.

Friday, February 8th.—The soldiers' committee has to-day decided to replace Pankratof by a Bolshevik commissary from Moscow. Things are going from bad to worse. It appears that there is no longer a state of war between Soviet Russia and Germany, Austria, and Bulgaria. The army is to be disbanded, but Lenin and Trotsky have not yet signed the peace.

Wednesday, February 13th.—The Czar tells me that the demobilisation of the army has begun, several classes having already been disbanded. All the old soldiers (the most friendly) are to leave us. The Czar seems very depressed at this prospect ; the change may have disastrous results for us.

Friday, February 15th.—A certain number of soldiers

have already left.   They came secretly to take leave of the Czar and his family.

At tea in the evening with Their Majesties, General Tatichtchef, with a frankness justified by the circumstances, expressed his surprise at finding how intimate and affectionate was the family life of the Czar and Czarina and their children.   The Czar, smiling at the Czarina, said, " You hear what Tatichtchef says ? "

Then, with his usual good-humour tinged with a touch of irony, he added :

" You have been my aide-de-camp, Tatichtchef, and had ever so many opportunities of observing us.   If you knew so little about us, how can you expect us to blame the newspapers for what they say about us ? "

Wednesday, February 20th.—The Czar tells me the Germans have taken Reval, Rovno, etc., and are still advancing along the whole front.   It is obvious that he is deeply affected.

Monday, February 25th.—Colonel Kobylinsky has received a telegram informing him that, from March 1st, " Nicholas Romanoff and his family must be put on *soldiers' rations* and that each member of the family will receive 600 roubles per month drawn from the interest of their personal estate."   Hitherto their expenses have been paid by the state.   As the family consists of seven persons, the whole household will have to be run on 4,200 roubles a month.[1]

Tuesday, February 26th.—His Majesty asked me to help him to do his accounts and draw up a family budget. He has saved a little from his " toilet allowance."

---

[1] At that time the value of the rouble was about one-fifth of the normal.

Wednesday, February 27th.—The Czar said jokingly that, since everyone is appointing committees, he is going to appoint one to look after the welfare of his own community. It is to consist of General Tatichtchef, Prince Dolgorouky, and myself. We held a " sitting " this afternoon and came to the conclusion that the *personnel* must be reduced. This is a wrench ; we shall have to dismiss ten servants, several of whom have their families with them in Tobolsk. When we informed Their Majesties we could see the grief it caused them. They must part with servants whose very devotion will reduce them to beggary.

Friday, March 1st.—The new régime comes into force. From to-day butter and coffee are excluded from the table as luxuries.

Monday, March 4th.—The soldiers' committee has decided to abolish the snow mountain we have built (it was such a source of amusement to the children !) because the Czar and Czarina mounted it to watch the departure of the men of the 4th Regiment. Every day now brings fresh vexations to the Czar's family and their suite. For a long time we have only been allowed to go out when accompanied by a soldier ; it is probable that even this last privilege will soon be taken from us.

Tuesday, March 5th.—Yesterday the soldiers, with a hang-dog look (for they felt it was a mean task), began to destroy the snow mountain with picks. The children are disconsolate.

Friday, March 15th.—The townspeople, hearing of our situation, find various ways of sending us eggs, sweetmeats, and delicacies.

Sunday, March 17th.—To-day is Carnival Sunday. Everyone is merry. The sledges pass to and fro under our windows; sound of bells, mouth-organs, and singing. . . . The children wistfully watch the fun. They have begun to grow bored and find their captivity irksome. They walk round the courtyard, fenced in by its high paling through which they can see nothing. Since the destruction of their snow mountain their only distraction is sawing and cutting wood.

The arrogance of the soldiers is inconceivable; those who have left have been replaced by a pack of black-guardly-looking young men.

In spite of the daily increase of their sufferings, Their Majesties still cherish hope that among their loyal friends some may be found to attempt their release. Never was the situation more favourable for escape, for there is as yet no representative of the Bolshevik Government at Tobolsk. With the complicity of Colonel Kobylinsky, already on our side, it would be easy to trick the insolent but careless vigilance of our guards. All that is required is the organised and resolute efforts of a few bold spirits outside. We have repeatedly urged upon the Czar the necessity of being prepared for any turn of events. He insists on two conditions which greatly complicate matters: he will not hear of the family being separated or leaving Russian territory.

One day the Czarina said to me in this connection: " I wouldn't leave Russia on any consideration, for it seems to me that to go abroad would be to break our last link with the past, which would then be dead for ever."

THE CZAR SAWING WOOD WITH ME. BEHIND, THE LITTLE GREEN-
HOUSE ON THE ROOF OF WHICH WE MADE TWO SEATS AT THE END OF
WINTER SO THAT WE COULD ENJOY THE SUN.

ALEXIS NICOLAÏEVITCH SITTING ON THE STEPS OF THE GOVERNOR'S
HOUSE. STANDING BY HIM IS THE SON OF DR. DEREVENKO, WHO
WAS ALLOWED TO COME AND PLAY WITH HIM WHEN WE FIRST WENT
TO TOBOLSK.

[*Facing page 256.*

Monday, March 18th.—During the first week of Lent the family will perform its devotions as usual. There is a service morning and evening. As their different occupations prevent the attendance of the choir, the Czarina and Grand-Duchesses sing with the deacon.

Tuesday, March 19th.—After lunch the Treaty of Brest-Litovsk was discussed. It has just been signed. The Czar was very depressed, saying : " It is such a disgrace for Russia and amounts to suicide. I should never have thought the Emperor William and the German Government could stoop to shake hands with these miserable traitors. But I'm sure they will get no good from it ; it won't save them from ruin ! "

A little later, when Prince Dolgorouky remarked that the newspapers were discussing a clause in which the Germans demanded that the Imperial family should be handed over to them unharmed, the Czar cried : " This is either a manœuvre to discredit me or an insult."

The Czarina added in a low voice : " After what they have done to the Czar, I would rather die in Russia than be saved by the Germans ! "

Friday, March 22nd.—At a quarter past nine, after the evening service, everyone went to Confession— children, servants, suite, and finally Their Majesties.

Saturday, March 23rd.—A detachment of over a hundred Red Guards has arrived from Omsk ; they are the first Maximalist soldiers to take up garrison duty at Tobolsk. Our last chance of escape has been snatched

R

from us. His Majesty, however, tells me he has reason to believe that there are among these men many officers who have enlisted in the ranks ; he also asserts, without telling me definitely the source of his information, that there are three hundred officers at Tioumen.

Tuesday, April 9th.—The Bolshevik commissary, who has come with the detachment from Omsk, has insisted on being allowed to inspect the house. The soldiers of our guard have refused permission. Colonel Kobylinsky is very uneasy and fears a conflict. Precautionary measures ; patrols, sentries doubled. A very disturbed night.

Wednesday, April 10th.—A " full sitting " of our guard, at which the Bolshevik commissary reveals the extent of his powers. He has the right to have anyone opposing his orders shot within twenty-four hours and without trial. The soldiers let him enter the house.

Friday, April 12th.—Alexis Nicolaïevitch confined to bed, as since yesterday he has had a violent pain in the groin caused by a strain. He has been so well this winter. It is to be hoped it is nothing serious.

A soldier of our detachment who had been sent to Moscow has returned to-day and brought Colonel Kobylinsky a memorandum from the Central Executive Committee of the Bolshevik Government, ordering him to be much stricter with us. General Tatichtchef, Prince Dolgorouky, and Countess Hendrikof are to be transferred to our house and treated as prisoners. The arrival is also announced of a commissary with extraordinary powers, accompanied by a detachment of soldiers.

Saturday, April 13th.—All who have been living in Kornilof's house, Countess Hendrikof, Mlle. Schneider, General Tatichtchef, Prince Dolgorouky, and Mr. Gibbes [1] move to our house. Only Doctors Botkin and Derevenko are left at liberty. Alexis Nicolaïevitch's pains have increased since yesterday.

Monday, April 15th.—Alexis Nicolaïvitch in great pain yesterday and to-day. It is one of his severe attacks of hæmophilia.

Tuesday, April 16th.—Colonel Kobylinsky, officer of the guard, and some soldiers have been to search the house. They have taken away the Czar's dagger which he wore with his Cossack uniform.

Monday, April 22nd.—The commissary from Moscow arrived to-day with a small detachment; his name is Yakovlef. He has shown his papers to the commandant and soldiers' committee. In the evening he took tea with Their Majesties. Everyone is restless and distraught. The commissary's arrival is felt to be an evil portent, vague but real.

Tuesday, April 23rd.—Commissary Yakovlef came at eleven o'clock. After an inspection of the whole house he went to see the Czar, who accompanied him to the room of Alexis Nicolaïevitch who is in bed. Not having been able to see the Czarina, who was not ready to receive him, he came again a little later with the regimental doctor and paid a second visit to Alexis Nicolaïevitch. (He wanted to be assured by his doctor that the boy was really ill.) As he was going

---

[1] My colleague Mr. Gibbes had joined us at Tobolsk during September.

away he asked the commandant whether we had much luggage. Can this mean we are to move ?

Wednesday, April 24th.—We are all in a state of mental anguish. We feel we are forgotten by everyone, abandoned to our own resources and at the mercy of this man. Is it possible that no one will raise a finger to save the Imperial family ? Where are those who have remained loyal to the Czar ? Why do they delay ?

Thursday, April 25th.—Shortly before three o'clock, as I was going along the passage, I met two servants sobbing. They told me that Yakovlef has come to tell the Czar that he is taking him away. What can be happening ? I dare not go up without being summoned, and went back to my room. Almost immediately Tatiana Nicolaïevna knocked at my door. She was in tears, and told me Her Majesty was asking for me. I followed her. The Czarina was alone, greatly upset. She confirmed what I had heard, that Yakovlef has been sent from Moscow to take the Czar away and is to leave to-night.

" The commissary says that no harm will come to the Czar, and that if anyone wishes to accompany him there will be no objection. I can't let the Czar go alone. They want to separate him from his family as they did before. . . .[1]

" They're going to try to force his hand by making him anxious about his family. . . . The Czar is necessary to them ; they feel that he alone represents Russia. . . . Together we shall be in a better position to resist them, and I ought to be at his side in the time

---

[1] The Czarina was alluding to the Czar's abdication.

AT THE MAIN DOOR OF THE GOVERNOR'S HOUSE DURING A WALK IN
THE COURT.

The four Grand-Duchesses. The Czarevitch. The officer of the Guard. The Czar.

THE CZARINA'S ROOM.
PICTURES OF THE CHILDREN ON THE WALL.

[*Facing page* **260**.

of trial. . . . But the boy is still so ill. . . . Suppose some complication sets in. . . . Oh, God, what ghastly torture ! . . . For the first time in my life I don't know what I ought to do ; I've always felt inspired whenever I've had to take a decision, and now I can't think. . . . But God won't allow the Czar's departure ; it can't, it *must* not be. I'm sure the thaw will begin to-night. . . ." [1]

Tatiana Nicolaïevna here intervened :

" But mother, if father has to go, whatever we say, something must be decided. . . ."

I took up the cudgels on Tatiana Nicolaïevna's behalf, remarking that Alexis Nicolaïevitch was better, and that we should take great care of him. . . .

Her Majesty was obviously tortured by indecision ; she paced up and down the room, and went on talking, rather to herself than to us. At last she came up to me and said :

" Yes, that will be best ; I'll go with the Czar ; I shall trust Alexis to you. . . ."

A moment later the Czar came in. The Czarina walked towards him, saying :

" It's settled ; I'll go with you, and Marie will come too."

The Czar replied : " Very well, if you wish it."

I came down to my room, and the whole day has been spent in getting ready. Prince Dolgorouky and Doctor Botkin will accompany Their Majesties, as also will Tchemadourof (the Czar's valet), Anna Demidova (the

---

[1] When the thaw set in the river was impassable for several days ; it was some time before the ferry could be re-started.

Czarina's maid), and Sednief (footman to the Grand-Duchesses). It has been decided that eight officers and men of our guard are to go with them.

The family have spent the whole afternoon at the bedside of Alexis Nicolaïevitch.

This evening at half-past ten we went up to take tea. The Czarina was seated on the divan with two of her daughters beside her. Their faces were swollen with crying. We all did our best to hide our grief and to maintain outward calm. We felt that for one to give way would cause all to break down. The Czar and Czarina were calm and collected. It is apparent that they are prepared for any sacrifices, even of their lives, if God in his inscrutable wisdom should require it for the country's welfare. They have never shown greater kindness or solicitude.

This splendid serenity of theirs, this wonderful faith, proved infectious.

At half-past eleven the servants were assembled in the large hall. Their Majesties and Marie Nicolaïevna took leave of them. The Czar embraced every man, the Czarina every woman. Almost all were in tears. Their Majesties withdrew; we all went down to my room.

At half-past three the conveyances drew up in the courtyard. They were the horrible *tarantass*.[1] Only one was covered. We found a little straw in the back-yard and spread it on the floor of the carriages. We put a mattress in the one to be used by the Czarina.

---

[1] Vehicles used by the peasants, and consisting of a large wicker basket hung from two long poles which take the place of springs. There are no seats; the passengers sit or lie on the floor.

At four o'clock we went up to see Their Majesties and found them just leaving Alexis Nicolaïevitch's room. The Czar and Czarina and Marie Nicolaïevna took leave of us. The Czarina and the Grand-Duchesses were in tears. The Czar seemed calm and had a word of encouragement for each of us ; he embraced us. The Czarina, when saying good-bye, begged me to stay upstairs with Alexis Nicolaïevitch. I went to the boy's room and found him in bed, crying.

A few minutes later we heard the rumbling of wheels. The Grand-Duchesses passed their brother's door on their way to their rooms, and I could hear them sobbing. . . .

Saturday, April 27th.—The man who drove the Czarina for the first stage has brought a note from Marie Nicolaïevna; the roads are founderous, travelling conditions terrible. How will the Czarina be able to stand the journey ? How heartrending it all is !

Sunday, April 28th.—Colonel Kobylinsky has received a telegram saying that the whole party arrived safely at Tioumen at half-past nine on Saturday evening.

The " field chapel " has been moved to the large hall, where the priest will be able to celebrate Mass, as there is a consecrated altar.

In the evening a second telegram arrived, sent after leaving Tioumen : " Travelling in comfort. How is the boy ? God be with you."

Monday, April 29th.—The children have received a letter from the Czarina from Tioumen. The journey has been very trying. Horses up to their chests in water crossing the rivers. Wheels broken several times.

Wednesday, May 1st.—Alexis Nicolaïevitch is up. Nagorny carried him to his wheeled chair; he was wheeled about in the sun.

Thursday, May 2nd.—Still no news since they left Tioumen. Where are they? They could have reached Moscow by Tuesday!

Friday, May 3rd.—Colonel Kobylinsky has received a telegram saying that the travellers have been detained at Ekaterinburg. What has happened?

Saturday, May 4th.—A sad Easter eve. We are in low spirits.

Sunday, May 5th.—Easter Day. Still no news.

Tuesday, May 7th.—At last the children have had a letter from Ekaterinburg saying that all are well but not explaining why they are held up. What agony can be read between the lines!

Wednesday, May 8th.—The officers and men of our guard who accompanied Their Majesties have returned from Ekaterinburg. They say that on arrival at Ekaterinburg the Czar's train was surrounded by Red Guards and that the Czar, Czarina, and Marie Nicolaïevna have been incarcerated in Ipatief's house. [1] Prince Dolgorouky is in prison, and they themselves were only released after two days' detention.

Saturday, May 11th.—Colonel Kobylinsky has been removed and we are left to the Tobolsk Soviet.

Friday, May 17th.—The soldiers of our guard have been replaced by Red Guards brought from Ekaterinburg by Commissary Rodionof, who has come to fetch us. General Tatichtchef and I both feel we ought to

---

[1] House belonging to a rich merchant of the town.

THE PRIEST CELEBRATING MASS IN THE DRAWING-ROOM OF THE
GOVERNOR'S HOUSE A FEW DAYS AFTER THE DEPARTURE OF THEIR
MAJESTIES. MAY, 1918.

THE RIVER STEAMER "ROUSS," ON WHICH THE CZAR AND HIS FAMILY
WERE CONVEYED FROM TIOUMEN TO TOBOLSK IN AUGUST, 1917, AND
THE CHILDREN FROM TOBOLSK TO TIOUMEN IN MAY, 1918.

[Facing page 264.

delay our departure as long as possible ; but the Grand-Duchesses are so eager to see their parents again that we don't feel morally justified in opposing their wishes.

Saturday, May 18th.—Vespers. The priest and nuns have been stripped and searched by order of the commissary.

Sunday, May 19th (May 6th, O.S.).—The Czar's birthday. . . . Our departure is fixed for to-morrow. The commissary refuses to allow the priest to come ; he has forbidden the Grand-Duchesses to lock their doors at night.

Monday, May 20th.—At half-past eleven we left the house and went on board the *Rouss*. She is the boat which brought us here with the Czar and Czarina eight months ago. Baroness Buxhœveden has been granted permission to rejoin us. We left Tobolsk at five o'clock. Commissary Rodionof has shut Alexis Nicolaïevitch in his cabin with Nagorny. We protested : the child is ill and the doctor ought to have access to him at any time.

Wednesday, May 22nd.—We reached Tioumen this morning.

CHAPTER XXI

EKATERINBURG

THE MURDER OF THE IMPERIAL FAMILY DURING THE NIGHT OF JULY 16-17TH, 1918

CHAPTER XXI

EKATERINBURG

THE MURDER OF THE IMPERIAL FAMILY DURING THE NIGHT OF JULY 16-17TH, 1918

ON our arrival at Tioumen on May 22nd we were at once taken, under a strong escort, to the special train that was to take us to Ekaterinburg. Just as I was getting into the train with my pupil I was separated from him and put in a fourth-class carriage, guarded by sentries like the others. We reached Ekaterinburg in the night, the train being stopped at some distance from the station.

About nine o'clock the next morning several carriages were drawn up alongside our train, and I saw four men go towards the children's carriage.

A few minutes passed and then Nagorny, the sailor attached to Alexis Nicolaïevitch, passed my window, carrying the sick boy in his arms; behind him came the Grand-Duchesses, loaded with valises and small personal belongings. I tried to get out, but was roughly pushed back into the carriage by the sentry.

I came back to the window. Tatiana Nicolaïevna came last, carrying her little dog and struggling to drag a heavy brown valise. It was raining, and I saw her feet sink into the mud at every step. Nagorny tried to come to her assistance; he was roughly pushed back by one of the commissaries. . . . A few minutes later the carriages drove off with the children in the direction of the town.

How little I suspected that I was never to see them again, after so many years among them! I was convinced that they would come back and fetch us and that we should be united without delay.

But the hours passed. Our train was shunted back into the station, and then I saw General Tatichtchef, Countess Hendrikof, and Mlle. Schneider being taken away. A little later it was the turn of Volkof, the Czarina's *valet-de-chambre*, de Kharitonof, the chef, Troup, the footman, and little Leonide Sednief, a kitchen boy of fourteen.

With the exception of Volkof, who managed to escape later, and little Sednief, whose life was spared, not one of those who were led off that day was destined to escape alive from the hands of the Bolsheviks.

We were still kept waiting. What was happening? Why didn't they come for us too? We gave ourselves up to all sorts of hypotheses, when, about five o'clock, Commissary Rodionof, who had come to Tobolsk to fetch us, entered our carriage and told us we were not wanted and were free.

Free! What was this? We were to be separated from the others? Then all was over! The excitement that had sustained us up to now gave place to deep depression. What was to be done? What was to be the next move? We were overwhelmed.

Even to-day I cannot understand what prompted the Bolsheviks to this decision to save our lives. Why, for instance, should Countess Hendrikof be taken to prison while Baroness de Buxhœveden, also a lady-in-waiting to the Czarina, was allowed to go free? Why they and not ourselves? Was there confusion of names or functions? A mystery!

On the next and following days I and my colleague went to

IPATIEF'S HOUSE AT EKATERINBURG, IN WHICH THE IMPERIAL FAMILY WERE INTERNED AND SUBSEQUENTLY MASSACRED.

Seen from the Vosnessensky Prospekt after the first fence had been erected.

[*Facing page* 270.

see the English and Swedish consuls [1]—the French consul was away; at all costs something had to be done to help the prisoners. The two consuls relieved our minds by telling us that proceedings had already been taken and that they did not think there was any imminent danger.

I walked past Ipatief's house, of which the tops of the windows could be seen above the wall of boards that hemmed it in. I had not yet lost all hope of effecting an entry, for Dr. Derevenko, who had been allowed to visit the boy, had heard Dr. Botkin ask Commissary Avdief, the commandant of the guard, on behalf of the Czar, that I should be allowed to rejoin them. Avdief had replied that he would refer the matter to Moscow. Meanwhile, my companions and I, except Dr. Derevenko, who had taken lodgings in the town, camped in the fourth-class carriage which had brought us. We were destined to remain there for more than a month !

On the twenty-sixth we were ordered to leave the territory of the Perm Government—which includes Ekaterinburg—without delay and return to Tobolsk. Care had been taken that we should only have one document between us, to keep us together and so facilitate supervision. But the trains were no longer running. The anti-Bolshevik movement of the Russian and Czech volunteers [2] was spreading rapidly, and the line was

---

1 I must pay a tribute to the very courageous conduct of the British consul, Mr. Preston, who did not shrink from open conflict with the Bolshevik authorities at the risk of compromising his personal safety.

2 In May, 1918, the Czecho-Slovakian troops (consisting of volunteers, former prisoners of war), who had by then been developed by Kerensky into two strong divisions, were strung along the Trans-Siberian railway between Samara and Vladivostok ; preparations were being made to pass them into France. The German G.H.Q., in an attempt to prevent these troops from rejoining the allied forces in Europe, ordered the Bolsheviks to disarm them. Following on an ultimatum that was rejected by the Czechs, fighting broke out between them and the Bolshevik troops under German officers. The Russian volunteer formations lost no time in joining up with the Czecho-Slovakian troops. Such was the origin of the movement which began at Omsk and soon spread over the whole of Siberia.

exclusively reserved for the military units that were being hurried to Tioumen.   This meant further delay.

One day when I was passing Ipatief's house, accompanied by Dr. Derevenko and Mr. Gibbes, we saw two carriages drawn up and surrounded by a large number of Red Guards. What was our horror at recognising in the first Sednief (the *valet-de-chambre* of the Grand-Duchesses) sitting between two guards.   Nagorny was going to the second carriage.   He was just setting foot on the step with his hand on the side of the carriage when, raising his head, he saw us all there standing motionless a few yards from him.   For a few seconds he looked fixedly at us, then, without a single gesture that might have betrayed us, he took his seat.   The carriages were driven off, and we saw them turn in the direction of the prison.

These two good fellows were shot shortly afterwards ; their sole crime had been their inability to hide their indignation on seeing the Bolshevik commissaries seize the little gold chain from which the holy images hung over the sick bed of Alexis Nicolaïevitch.

A few more days passed, and then I learned through Dr. Derevenko that the request made on my behalf had been refused.

On June 3rd our carriage was coupled to one of the many trains loaded with starving people from Russia coming to look for food in Siberia. We made for Tioumen, where, after various wanderings, we finally arrived on the fifteenth   A few hours later I was placed under arrest by Bolshevik headquarters, where I had been forced to apply for a *visa* that was indispensable to my companions and myself.   It was only by a lucky combination of circumstances that I came to be released in the evening and was able to get back to the railway carriage, in

YOUROVSKY, FROM A PHOTOGRAPH PRODUCED AT THE ENQUIRY.

THE GRAND-DUCHESSES' ROOM AS I SAW IT ON ENTERING IPATIEF'S
HOUSE. ON THE FLOOR ARE THE ASHES FROM THE STOVES.

[Facing page 272.

which they were waiting for me. The following days were days of indescribable anxiety, at the mercy of any chance that might call attention to us. Probably what saved us was that we were lost in the crowd of refugees who filled Tioumen station, and so managed to pass unnoticed.

On July 20th the Whites, as the anti-Bolshevik troops were called, captured Tioumen and saved us from the fanatics who had so nearly claimed us as victims. A few days later the papers published a reproduction of the proclamation that had been placarded in the streets of Ekaterinburg, announcing that the sentence of death passed on the ex-Czar Nicholas Romanoff had been carried out on the night of July 16th-17th and that the Czarina and her children had been removed to a place of safety.

At last, on July 25th, Ekaterinburg fell in its turn. Hardly was communication re-established—which took a long time as the permanent way had suffered severely—when Mr. Gibbes and I hastened to the town to search for the Imperial family and those of our companions who had remained at Ekaterinburg.

Two days after my arrival I made my first entry into Ipatief's house. I went through the first-floor rooms, which had served as the prison ; they were in an indescribable state of disorder. It was evident that every effort had been made to get rid of any traces of the recent occupants. Heaps of ashes had been raked out of the stoves. Among them were a quantity of small articles, half burnt, such as tooth-brushes, hairpins, buttons, etc., in the midst of which I found the end of a hair-brush on the browned ivory of which could still be seen the initials of the Czarina, A. F. (Alexandra-Feodorovna). If it was true that the prisoners had been sent away, they

S

must have been removed just as they were, without any of the most essential articles of toilet.

I then noticed on the wall in the embrasure of one of the windows of Their Majesties' room the Empress's favourite charm, the swastika,[1] which she had put up everywhere to ward off ill-luck. She had drawn it in pencil, and added, underneath, the date, 17/30 April, the day of their incarceration in the house. The same symbol, but without the date, was drawn on the wallpaper, on a level with the bed, occupied doubtless by her or Alexis Nicolaïevitch. But my search was to no purpose, I could not find the slightest clue to their fate.

I went down to the bottom floor, the greater part of which was below the level of the ground. It was with intense emotion that I entered the room in which perhaps—I was still in doubt—they had met their death. Its appearance was sinister beyond expression. The only light filtered through a barred window at the height of a man's head. The walls and floor showed numerous traces of bullets and bayonet scars. The first glance showed that an odious crime had been perpetrated there and that several people had been done to death. But who? How?

I became convinced that the Czar had perished and, granting that, I could not believe that the Czarina had survived him. At Tobolsk, when Commissary Yakovlef had come to take away the Czar, I had seen her throw herself in where the danger seemed to her greatest. I had seen her, broken-hearted after hours of mental torture, torn desperately between her feelings as a wife and a mother, abandon her sick boy to follow the husband whose life seemed in danger. Yes, it was possible

---

[1] The swastika is an Indian religious symbol consisting of a cross of equal limbs, their extremities bent to the left.

they might have died together, the victims of these brutes. But the children ? They too massacred ? I could not believe it. My whole being revolted at the idea. And yet everything proved that there had been many victims. Well, then ? . . .

During the following days I continued my investigations in Ekaterinburg and its suburbs—the monastery, everywhere I could hope to find the slightest clue. I saw Father Storojef, who had been the last to conduct religious service in Ipatief's house, on Sunday, the 14th, two days before the night of terror. He too, alas, had very little hope.

The enquiry proceeded very slowly. It was begun in extremely difficult circumstances, for, between July 17th and 25th the Bolshevik commissaries had had time to efface nearly every trace of their crime. Immediately after the taking of Ekaterinburg by the Whites, the military authorities had surrounded the house with a guard and a judicial enquiry had been opened, but the threads had been so skilfully entangled that it was very difficult to sort them out.

The most important deposition was that of some peasants from the village of Koptiaki, twenty versts north-west of Ekaterinburg. They came to give evidence that on the night of July 16th-17th the Bolsheviks had occupied a clearing in a forest near their village, where they had remained several days. They brought with them objects which they had found near the shaft of an abandoned mine, not far from which could be seen traces of a large fire. Some officers visited the clearing and found other objects, which, like the first, were recognised as having belonged to the Imperial family.

The enquiry had been entrusted to Ivan Alexandrovitch Serguéief, a member of the Ekaterinburg tribunal. It followed a normal course, but the difficulties were very great.

Serguéief was more and more inclined to admit the death of all the members of the family. But the bodies could still not be found, and the depositions of a certain number of witnesses supported the hypothesis that the Czarina and the children had been removed to another place. These depositions—as was subsequently established—emanated from Bolshevik agents deliberately left in Ekaterinburg to mislead the enquiry. Their end was partially attained, for Serguéief lost precious time and was long in realising that he was on the wrong track.

The weeks passed without bringing any new information. I then decided to return to Tioumen, the cost of living at Ekaterinburg being very high. Before starting, however, I obtained from Serguéief a promise that he would recall me if any new fact of importance came to light in the course of the enquiry.

At the end of January, 1919, I received a telegram from General Janin, whom I had known at Mohilef when he was chief of the French Military Mission at Russian G.H.Q. He invited me to join him at Omsk. Some days later I left Tioumen, and on February 13th arrived at the Military Mission sent by France to the Omsk Government.[1]

Admiral Koltchak, realising the historic importance of the enquiry into the disappearance of the Imperial family, and wishing to know the result, had in January charged General Ditériks to bring him from Ekaterinburg a copy of the evidence and all the clues that had been found. On February 5th he summoned Nicholas Alexiévitch Sokolof, " Examining

---

[1] The Allies had resolved to exploit the anti-Bolshevik movement which had developed in Siberia and to make immediate use of the Czecho-Slovakian troops by creating on the Volga a new front against the Germano-Bolshevik troops, which might create a diversion and hold back part of the German forces freed by the treaty of Brest-Litovsk. Hence the despatch by France and England of civil and military missions to Siberia. The anti-Bolshevik Government of Omsk was at that time controlled by Admiral Koltchak.

IPATIEF'S HOUSE, FROM THE VOSNESSENSKY STREET.

On the ground floor, the window between two trees is that of the room in which the murders took place. Above it is the window of the Grand-Duchesses' room. The four windows in pairs at the angle of the upper floor are those of the room occupied by the Czar, the Czarina, and the Czarevitch.

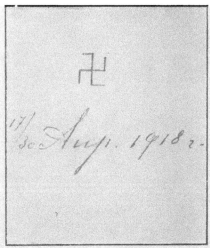

THE CZARINA'S FAVOURITE LUCKY CHARM, THE "SWASTIKA," WHICH SHE DREW IN THE EMBRASURE OF ONE OF THE WINDOWS IN HER ROOM AT EKATERINBURG, ADDING THE DATE, 17/30 APRIL, 1918.

On the left, photograph of the inscription under glass with four seals. On the right, the inscription.

Magistrate,"[1] for business of particular importance, and invited him to conduct the enquiry. Two days later the Minister of Justice appointed him to carry on Serguéief's work.

It was at this juncture that I made the acquaintance of M. Sokolof. At our first interview I realised that his mind was made up and that he had no further hope. I could not believe such horrors. " But the children—the children ? " I cried to him. " The children have suffered the same fate as their parents. There is not a shadow of doubt in my mind on that point." " But the bodies ? " " The clearing must be searched ; that is where we shall find the key to the mystery, for the Bolsheviks cannot have spent three days and nights here simply to burn a few clothes."

Alas ! these conclusions were soon to be borne out by the deposition of one of the principal murderers, Paul Medvedief, who had just been taken prisoner at Perm. As Sokolof was at Omsk it was Serguéief who interrogated him on February 25th at Ekaterinburg. He admitted formally that the Czar, Czarina and the five children, Dr. Botkin, and the three servants had been killed in the basement of Ipatief's house during the night of July 16th-17th. He could not, however, or would not, give any hint as to what had been done with the bodies after the murder.

I worked for several days with M. Sokolof ; then he left for Ekaterinburg to continue the enquiry opened by Serguéief.

In April, General Ditériks, who was returning from Vladivostok—where he had been sent by Admiral Koltchak on a special mission—came to join him and assist his efforts. Thenceforward the enquiry made rapid progress. Hundreds

---

[1] There were three categories of Examining Magistrates : (a) Examining Magistrates for ordinary business ; (b) Examining Magistrates for important business ; (c) Examining Magistrates for business of particular importance.

of persons were interrogated, and, as soon as the snow had gone, work was begun on a large scale in the clearing in which the Koptiaki peasants had found articles belonging to the Imperial family.   The mine-shaft was emptied and thoroughly examined.   The ashes and soil of part of the clearing were passed through sieves, and the whole of the surrounding area carefully examined.   They succeeded in determining the site of two large fires and, more vaguely, the traces of a third. This methodical research soon brought discoveries of extreme importance.

Devoting himself wholeheartedly to the work he had undertaken, and displaying untiring patience and diligence, M. Sokolof was able in a few months to reconstruct every circumstance of the crime with remarkable accuracy.

CHAPTER XXII

THE CIRCUMSTANCES OF THE CRIME ESTABLISHED BY THE ENQUIRY

CHAPTER XXII

THE CIRCUMSTANCES OF THE CRIME
ESTABLISHED BY THE ENQUIRY

IN the following pages I shall describe the circumstances of the murder of the Imperial family as they appear from the depositions of the witnesses and evidence examined by the enquiry. From the six thick manuscript volumes in which it is contained I have extracted the essential facts of this drama about which, alas! there can be no longer any doubt. The impression left by reading these documents is that of a ghastly nightmare, but I do not feel justified in dwelling on the horror.

About the middle of May, 1918, Yankel Sverdlof, President of the Central Executive Committee at Moscow, yielding to the pressure of Germany,[1] sent Commissary Yakovlef to Tobolsk to arrange for the transfer of the Imperial family. He had received orders to take them to Moscow or Petrograd. In carrying out his mission he met with resistance which he did his best to overcome, as the enquiry has established. This resistance had been organised by the divisional government of the Ural, whose headquarters were at Ekaterinburg. It was they who, unknown to Yakovlef, prepared the trap which enabled them to seize the Emperor *en route*. But it appears

---

[1] Germany's aim was the restoration of the monarchy in favour of the Czar or Czarevitch, on condition that the treaty of Brest-Litovsk was recognised and Russia should become Germany's ally. This plan failed, thanks to the resistance of the Czar Nicholas II., who was probably the victim of his fidelity to his allies.

to have been established that this plan had been secretly approved by Moscow.   It is more than probable, indeed, that Sverdlof was playing a double game, and that, while pretending to accede to the pressure of General Baron von Mirbach in Moscow, he had arranged with the Ekaterinburg commissaries not to let the Czar escape.   However this may be, the installation of the Czar at Ekaterinburg was carried out on the spur of the moment.   In two days the merchant Ipatief was evicted from his house and the construction of a strong wooden fencing rising to the level of the second-floor windows begun.

To this place the Czar, Czarina, Grand-Duchess Marie Nicolaïevna, Dr. Botkin, and three servants accompanying them were brought on April 30th.   Also Anna Demidova, the Czarina's maid, Tchemadourof, the Czar's valet, and Sednief, the Grand-Duchesses' footman.

At first the guard was formed by soldiers picked at random and frequently changed.   Later it consisted exclusively of workmen from the Sissert workshops and the factory of Zlokazof Brothers.   They were under the command of Commissary Avdief, commandant of the " house destined for a special purpose," as Ipatief's house was named.

The conditions of the imprisonment were much more severe than at Tobolsk.   Avdief was an inveterate drunkard, who gave rein to his coarse instincts, and, with the assistance of his subordinates, showed great ingenuity in daily inflicting fresh humiliations upon those in his charge.   There was no alternative but to accept the privations, submit to the vexations, yield to the exactions and caprices of these low, vulgar scoundrels.

On their arrival in Ekaterinburg on May 23rd, the Czarevitch and his three sisters were at once taken to Ipatief's house,

THE ROOM ON THE GROUND FLOOR OF IPATIEF'S HOUSE IN WHICH THE IMPERIAL FAMILY AND THEIR COMPANIONS WERE PUT TO DEATH.

[Facing page 282.

where their parents were awaiting them. After the agony of separation this reunion was a tremendous joy, in spite of the sadness of the present and the uncertainty of the future.

A few hours later Kharitonof (the chef), old Troup (footman), and little Leonide Sednief (scullery-boy) were also brought. General Tatichtchef, Countess Hendrikof, Mlle. Schneider, and Volkof, the Czarina's *valet-de-chambre*, had been taken direct to the prison.

On the twenty-fourth, Tchemadourof, who had been taken ill, was transferred to the prison hospital; there he was forgotten, and so, miraculously, escaped death. A few days later Nagorny and Sednief were also removed. The number of those who had been left with the prisoners decreased rapidly. Fortunately Dr. Botkin, whose devotion was splendid, was left, and also a few servants whose faithfulness was proof against anything: Anna Demidova, Kharitonof, Troup, and little Leonide Sednief. During these days of suffering the presence of Dr. Botkin was a great comfort to the prisoners; he did all he could for them, acted as intermediary between them and the commissaries, and did his best to protect them against the coarse insults of their guards.

The Czar, Czarina, and Czarevitch occupied the room in the angle formed by the square and Vosnessensky Lane; the four Grand-Duchesses the adjoining room, the door of which had been removed; at first, as there was no bed, they slept on the floor. Dr. Botkin slept in the drawing-room and the Czarina's maid in the room in the angle of Vosnessensky Lane and the garden. The other prisoners were installed in the kitchen and adjacent hall.

Alexis Nicolaïevitch's ill-health had been aggravated by

the fatigue of the journey; he spent the greater part of the day lying down, and when they went out to take the air it was the Czar who carried him as far as the garden.

The family and servants took their meals with the commissaries, who occupied the same floor as themselves, and so lived in constant proximity with these coarse men, who more often than not were drunk.

The house had been surrounded by a second fence of boards; it had been turned into a veritable prison fortress. There were sentries stationed outside and within, machine-guns in the building and garden. The room of the Commissary Commandant—the first on entering the house—was occupied by Commissary Avdief, his adjutant Mochkine, and some workmen. The rest of the guard lived in the basement, but the men often came upstairs and strolled into the rooms of the Imperial family as they liked. The courage of the prisoners was, however, sustained in a remarkable way by religion. They had kept that wonderful faith which at Tobolsk had been the admiration of their *entourage* and which had given them such strength, such serenity in suffering. They were already almost entirely detached from this world. The Czarina and Grand-Duchesses could often be heard singing religious airs, which affected their guards in spite of themselves.

Gradually these guards were humanised by contact with their prisoners. They were astonished at their simplicity, attracted by their gentleness, subdued by their serene dignity, and soon found themselves dominated by those whom they thought they held in their power. The drunken Avdief found himself disarmed by such greatness of soul; he grew conscious of his own infamy. The early ferocity of these men was succeeded by profound pity.

The Soviet authorities in Ekaterinburg comprised :

(a) *The Divisional Council of the Urals*, consisting of about thirty members under the presidency of Commissary Bieloborodof.

(b) *The Presidium*, a sort of executive committee of several members : Bieloborodof, Golochtchokine, Syromolotof, Safarof, Voïkof, etc.

(c) *The Tchrezvytchaïka*. The popular title of the " Extraordinary Commission for Combating Counter-Revolution and Speculation," with its centre at Moscow and branches throughout Russia. This is a formidable organisation which is the very foundation of the Soviet régime. Each section receives its orders direct from Moscow and carries them out through its own resources. Every *Tchrezvytchaïka* of any importance commands the services of a band of nondescript agents, generally Austro-German prisoners of war, Letts, Chinese, etc., who are in reality nothing more than highly-paid executioners.

In Ekaterinburg the *Tchrezvytchaïka* was all-powerful. Its most influential members were Commissaries Yourovsky, Golochtchokine, etc.

Avdief was under the immediate control of the other commissaries, members of the *Presidium* and *Tchrezvytchaïka*. They were not long in realising the change which had come about in the feelings of the guards towards their prisoners, and resolved to adopt drastic measures. At Moscow, too, there was uneasiness, as was proved by the following telegram sent from Ekaterinburg by Bieloborodof to Sverdlof and Golochtchokine (who was then at Moscow) : " Syromolotof just left for Moscow to organise according to instructions from centre.

Anxiety unnecessary. Useless to worry. Avdief revoked. Mochkine arrested. Avdief replaced by Yourovsky. Inside guard changed, replaced by others."

This telegram is dated July 4th.

On this day Avdief and his adjutant Mochkine were arrested and replaced by Commissary Yourovsky, a Jew, and his subordinate Nikouline. The guard formed—as has already been mentioned—exclusively of Russian workmen, was transferred to a neighbouring house, that of Popof.

Yourovsky brought with him ten men—nearly all Austro-German prisoners of war—" selected " from among the executioners of the *Tchrezvytchaïka*. Henceforward these formed the inside guard, the outside sentries being still furnished by the Russian guard.

The " house destined for a special purpose " had become a branch of the *Tchrezvytchaïka*, and the lives of the prisoners became one long martyrdom.

At this time the death of the Imperial family had already been decided upon in Moscow. The telegram quoted above proves this. Syromolotof left for Moscow " to organise according to instructions from centre "; he was to return with Golochtchokine, bringing instructions and directions from Sverdlof. Meanwhile Yourovsky made his arrangements. On several days in succession he went out on horseback. He was seen wandering about the neighbourhood looking for a place suitable for his plans, in which he could dispose of the bodies of his victims. And this same man, with inconceivable cynicism, on his return visited the bedside of the Czarevitch !

Several days pass ; Golochtchokine and Syromolotof have come back. All is ready.

MINE-SHAFT WHERE THE ASHES WERE THROWN.

THE SEARCH IN THE MINE-SHAFT.

[Facing page 256.

On Sunday, July 14th, Yourovsky summons a priest, Father Storojef, and authorises a religious service. The prisoners are already condemned to death and must not be refused the succour of religion.

The next day he gives orders for the removal of little Leonide Sednief to Popof's house, where the Russian guard are quartered.

On the sixteenth, about 7 p.m., he orders Paul Medvedief, in whom he has every confidence—Medvedief was in control of the Russian workmen—to bring him the twelve Nagan revolvers with which the Russian guard are armed. When this order has been carried out he tells him that all the Imperial family will be put to death that same night, directing him to inform the Russian guard later. Medvedief informs them about 10 p.m.

Shortly after midnight, Yourovsky enters the rooms occupied by the members of the Imperial family, wakes them up, together with their *entourage*, and tells them to get ready to follow him. The pretext he alleges is that they are to be taken away, that there are disturbances in the town, and meanwhile they will be safer on the floor below.

Everyone is soon ready. They take a few small belongings and some cushions and then go down by the inner staircase leading to the court from which they enter the ground-floor rooms. Yourovsky goes in front with Nikouline, followed by the Czar, carrying Alexis Nicolaïevitch, the Czarina, the Grand-Duchesses, Dr. Botkin, Anna Demidova, Kharitonof, and Troup.

The prisoners remain in the room indicated by Yourovsky. They are persuaded that the carriages or cars which are to take them away are being fetched, and as the wait may be long they ask for chairs. Three are brought. The Czarevitch, who cannot stand because of his leg, sits down in the middle of the room. The Czar takes his place on his left, Dr. Botkin standing on his right a little to the rear. The Czarina sits down near the wall (to the right of the door by which they entered), not far from the window. A cushion has been placed on her chair and that of Alexis Nicolaïevitch. Behind her she has one of her daughters, probably Tatiana. In the corner on the same side Anna Demidova—still holding two cushions in her arms. The three other Grand-Duchesses are standing with their backs to the wall furthest from the door, and in the corner to their right are Kharitonof and old Troup.

The wait is prolonged. Suddenly Yourovsky re-enters the room with seven Austro-Germans and two of his friends, Commissaries Ermakof and Vaganof, accredited executioners of the *Tchrezvytchaïka*. Medvedief is also present. Yourovsky comes forward and says to the Czar : " Your men have tried to save you but haven't succeeded, and we are forced to put you to death." He immediately raises his revolver and fires point-blank at the Czar, who falls dead. This is the signal for a general discharge of revolvers. Each of the murderers has chosen his victim. Yourovsky has reserved for himself the Czar and Czarevitch. For most of the prisoners death is instantaneous. But Alexis Nicolaïevitch is moaning feebly. Yourovsky finishes him off with a shot from his revolver. Anastasie Nicolaïevna is only wounded, and begins to scream as the murderers approach ; she is killed by their bayonets. Anna Demidova, too, has been spared, thanks to the cushions which she holds in front of her. She rushes about, and finally falls under the bayonets of the assassins.

The depositions of the witnesses have made it possible for the enquiry to reconstruct the ghastly scene of the massacre in all its details. These witnesses are Paul Medvedief,[1] one of the murderers ; Anatole Yakimof, who was certainly present at the drama, although he denies it, and Philip Proskouriakof, who describes the crime from the story of other spectators. All three were members of the guard at Ipatief's house.

When all is over, the commissaries remove from the victims their jewels, and the bodies are carried, with the help of sheets and the shafts of a sledge, to a motor-wagon which is waiting at the courtyard door, between the two wooden fences.

They have to hurry for fear of the dawn. The funeral procession crosses the still-sleeping town and makes for the forest. Commissary Vaganof rides ahead, as a chance encounter must be avoided. Just as they are approaching the clearing for which they are making, he sees a wagon driven by peasants coming towards him. It is a woman of the village of Koptiaki, who set out in the night with her son and daughter-in-law to sell fish in the town. He orders them to turn round and go home. To make doubly sure he goes with them, galloping alongside the cart, and forbids them under pain of death to turn round or look behind them. But the peasant woman has had time to catch a glimpse of the great dark object coming up behind the horseman. When she gets back to the village she tells what she has seen. The puzzled peasants start out to reconnoitre, and run into a cordon of sentries stationed in the forest.

---

[1] Medvedief was taken prisoner at the capture of Perm by the anti-Bolshevik troops in February, 1919. He died a month later at Ekaterinburg of exanthematic typhus. He claimed to have been present at only part of the drama and not to have fired himself. (Other witnesses affirm the contrary.) It is the classic defence of all the assassins.

T

However, after great difficulties, for the roads are very bad, the motor-wagon reaches the clearing. The bodies are placed on the ground and partly undressed. It is then that· the commissaries discover a quantity of jewellery that the Grand-Duchesses carry concealed under their clothes. They at once seize them, but, in their haste, let a few fall on the ground, where they are trodden into the soil. The bodies are then cut in pieces and placed on great bonfires, which are made to burn more fiercely by the application of benzine. The parts which resist the flames are destroyed with sulphuric acid. For three days and three nights the murderers toil at their labour of destruction under the direction of Yourovsky and his two friends Ermakof and Vaganof. One hundred and seventy-five kilogrammes of sulphuric acid and more than 300 litres of benzine are brought to the clearing.

At last, on July 20th, all is finished. The murderers efface all traces of the fires, and the ashes are thrown into a mine-shaft or scattered about the neighbourhood of the clearing, so that nothing may reveal what has taken place.

.   .   .   .   .   .

Why did these men take so much trouble to efface all traces of their deed ?   Why, since they professed to be acting as the servants of justice, did they hide like criminals ?   And from whom were they hiding ?

It is Paul Medvedief who explains this in his evidence. After the crime Yourovsky came up to him and said, " Keep the outside sentries at their posts in case there is trouble with the people ! " And during the following days the sentries continued to mount guard round the empty house as if nothing had happened, as if the fences still shut in the prisoners.

M. SOKOLOFF EXAMINING THE ASHES OF THE FIRE NEAREST TO THE
MINE-SHAFT.

M. SOKOLOFF EXAMINING THE TRACES OF ONE OF THE FIRES AT THE
FOOT OF AN OLD PINE.

[*Facing page* 290.

Those who must be deceived, must not know, are the *Russian people*.

Another fact proves this : the precaution taken on July 4th of sending away Avdief and the Russian guard. The commissaries no longer had confidence in these workmen from the Sissert workshops and the factory of Zlokazof, who had, however, rallied to their cause and enlisted voluntarily to guard " bloody Nicholas." They knew that none but paid assassins, convicts, or foreigners would consent to carry through the infamous task they were proposing. These assassins were Yourovsky (a Jew), Medvedief, Nikouline, Ermakof, Vaganof, Russian convicts, and seven Austro-Germans.

Yes, it was from the Russian people that they were hiding, the men whose agents they professed to be. It was of them they were afraid ; of their vengeance.

At last, on July 20th, they decided to speak and announce the death of the Emperor to the people in a proclamation published in the following form :

DECISION

OF THE PRESIDIUM OF THE DIVISIONAL COUNCIL OF DEPUTIES OF WORKMEN, PEASANTS, AND RED GUARDS OF THE URALS :

In view of the fact that Czecho-Slovakian bands are threatening the Red capital of the Urals, Ekaterinburg ; that the crowned executioner may escape from the tribunal of the people (a White Guard plot to carry off the whole Imperial family has just been discovered), the Presidium of the Divisional Committee, in pursuance of the will of the people, has decided that the ex-Czar

Nicholas Romanoff, guilty before the people of innumerable bloody crimes, shall be shot.

The decision of the Presidium of the Divisional Council was carried into execution on the night of July 16th-17th.

Romanoff's family has been transferred from Ekaterinburg to a place of greater safety.

THE PRESIDIUM OF THE DIVISIONAL COUNCIL
OF DEPUTIES OF WORKMEN, PEASANTS, AND
RED GUARDS OF THE URALS.

DECISION

OF THE PRESIDIUM OF THE CENTRAL EXECUTIVE COMMITTEE OF ALL THE RUSSIAS OF JULY 18TH, a.c.

The Central Executive Committee of the Councils of Deputies of Workmen, Peasants, Red Guards, and Cossacks, in the person of their president, approve the action of the Presidium of the Council of the Urals.

The President of the Central Executive Committee,
Y. SVERDLOF.

In this document mention is made of the sentence of death passed, it is alleged, by the *Presidium* of Ekaterinburg, on the Czar Nicholas II. A lie! The crime, we know, was decided on in Moscow by Sverdlof, his instructions being brought to Yourovsky by Golochtchokine and Syromolotof.

Sverdlof was the head and Yourovsky the arm; both were Jews.

The Czar was neither condemned nor even judged—and by whom could he have been?—he was assassinated. And what of the Czarina, the children, Dr. Botkin, and the three servants who died with them ?   But what does it matter to the murderers ?   They are sure of impunity ; the bullet killed, the flame destroyed, and the earth covered what the fire could not devour.   Oh, they are very easy in their minds ; no one will talk, for they are united by infamy.   And it seems to be with reason that Commissary Voïkof can exclaim, " The world will never know what we have done with them ! "

These men were mistaken.

After months of groping, the enquiry commission undertook methodical investigation in the forest.   Every inch of ground was searched, scrutinised, examined, and soon the mineshaft, the soil of the clearing, and the grass of the vicinity revealed their secret.   Hundreds of articles and fragments, for the most part trodden into the ground, were discovered, identified, and classified by the court of enquiry.   Amongst other things, they found in this way :

The buckle of the Czar's belt, a fragment of his cap, the little portable frame containing the portrait of the Czarina— the photograph had disappeared—which the Czar always carried about him, etc.

The Czarina's favourite ear-rings (one broken), pieces of her dress, the glass of her spectacles, recognisable by its special shape, etc.

The buckle of the Czarevitch's belt, some buttons, and pieces of his cloak, etc.

A number of small articles belonging to the Grand-Duchesses : fragments of necklaces, shoes, buttons, hooks, press-buttons, etc.

Six metal corset busks. " Six "—a number which speaks for

itself when the number of the female victims is remembered :
the Czarina, the four Grand-Duchesses, and A. Demidova,
the Czarina's maid.

Dr. Botkin's false teeth, fragments of his eyeglasses,
buttons from his clothes, etc.

Finally charred bones and fragments of bones, partly
destroyed by acid and occasionally bearing the mark of a
sharp instrument or saw ; revolver bullets—doubtless those
which had remained embedded in the bodies—and a fairly
large quantity of melted lead.

A pathetic list of relics, leaving, alas ! no hope, and showing
up the truth in all its brutality and horror. Commissary
Voïkof was mistaken : the world now knows what they did
with them.

Meanwhile the murderers were growing uneasy. The
agents they had left at Ekaterinburg to set the enquiry on
false trails kept them in touch with its progress. This they
followed step by step. And when they understood finally that
the truth was about to be revealed, that the whole world would
soon know what had happened, they became afraid, and tried
to throw on to others the responsibility for their crime. It
was then that they accused the socialist-revolutionaries of
being the authors of the crime and of having tried this means of
compromising the Bolshevik party. In September, 1919,
twenty-eight persons were arrested by them at Perm, falsely
accused of having participated in the murder of the Imperial
family, and tried. Five of them were condemned to death
and executed.

This odious farce forms one more illustration of the cynicism
of these men who did not hesitate to send innocent people to

DR. BOTKIN, WHO WAS KILLED WITH THE IMPERIAL FAMILY.

GROUP TAKEN AT TOBOLSK, WHEN WE WERE COMPELLED TO BE
PHOTOGRAPHED.

Left to right, in front : Mlle. Schneider and Countess Hendrikof (shot at Perm).
Behind : General Tatichtchef (shot at Ekaterinburg), the author, Prince Dolgorouky
(shot at Ekaterinburg).

[*Facing page* 294.

their death rather than incur the responsibility for one of the greatest crimes of history.

.   .   .   .   .   .

It remains to mention the tragedy of Alapaevsk, which is closely connected with that of Ekaterinburg, and caused the death of several other members of the Imperial family.

The Grand-Duchess Elizabeth Feodorovna, sister of the Czarina, the Grand-Duke Sergius Michaïlovitch, cousin of the Czar, Princes Jean, Constantin, and Igor, sons of the Grand-Duke Constantin, and Prince Palée, son of the Grand-Duke Paul, had been arrested in the spring of 1918 and taken to the little town of Alapaevsk, situated 150 versts north of Ekaterinburg. A nun, Barbe Yakovlef, the Grand-Duchess's companion, and S. Remes, secretary of the Grand-Duke Sergius, shared their captivity. Their prison was the school-house.

In the night of July 17th-18th, twenty-four hours after the Ekaterinburg crime, they were fetched and, under pretext of being removed to another town, were driven about twelve versts from Alapaevsk. There, in a forest, they were put to death. Their bodies were thrown into the shaft of an abandoned mine, where they were found, in October, 1918, covered with the earth thrown up by the explosion of hand-grenades by which the sufferings of the victims had been terminated.

The autopsy revealed traces of death by shooting only on the body of the Grand-Duke Sergius, and the enquiry has failed to establish exactly how his companions were killed. It is probable that they were beaten down with rifle-butts.

This crime of unexampled brutality was the work of Commissary Safarof, member of the Ekaterinburg *Presidium*, who, however, was acting entirely on the orders of Moscow.

.   .   .   .   .

Some days after the capture of Ekaterinburg, when order was being restored in the town and the dead buried, two bodies were found not far from the prison. On one of them was found a receipt for 80,000 roubles made out to Citizen Dolgorouky, and, according to the descriptions of witnesses, it seems certain that this was the body of Prince Dolgorouky. There is every reason to believe that the other was the body of General Tatichtchef.

Both died, as they had expected, for their Czar. General Tatichtchef said to me one day at Tobolsk : " I know I shan't come out alive. I only ask one thing, not to be separated from the Czar and to be allowed to die with him." Even this supreme consolation was denied him.

Countess Hendrikof and Mlle. Schneider were removed from Ekaterinburg a few days after the murder of the Imperial family and taken to Perm. There they were shot in the night of September 3rd-4th, 1918. Their bodies were found and identified in May, 1919.

As for Nagorny, Alexis Nicolaïevitch's sailor, and the footman, Ivan Sednief, they were put to death in the neighbourhood of Ekaterinburg in the beginning of June, 1918. Their bodies were found two months later at the place of execution.

All, from General to seaman, did not hesitate to sacrifice their lives and go bravely to meet death. This seaman, however, a humble peasant from the Ukraine, had only to say one word to be saved. He had only to deny his Czar. This word remained unspoken.

For a long time, with simple and sincere faith, they had devoted their lives to those they loved, who had been able to inspire those who surrounded them with so much affection, courage, and self-sacrifice.

EPILOGUE

EPILOGUE

THE summer of 1919 was marked by the great reverses which were to bring, a few months later, the downfall of Admiral Koltchak's government. The Bolshevik troops had retaken Perm and were threatening Ekaterinburg. The work undertaken in the clearing at Koptiaki had to be abandoned before its completion. On July 12th, N. Sokolof, heartbroken, decided to leave for Omsk. There he spent the month of August, and then, seeing that the situation was growing still worse, he went on to Tchita, whilst I remained at Omsk.

A few weeks after his departure, two Russian officers came to the French Military Mission and asked to speak to me. They told me that General D—— had an important communication to make to me, and begged me to be so kind as to go and see him. We got into the car which was waiting, and a few moments later I found myself in his presence.

General D—— informed me that he wanted to show me a boy who claimed to be the Czarevitch. I knew in fact that a rumour was spreading in Omsk that the Czarevitch was still alive. He was announced to be in a small town of Altaï. I had been told that the inhabitants had greeted him with enthusiasm; the schoolchildren had made a collection on his behalf, and the governor of the station had offered him, on his knees, bread and salt. In addition, Admiral Koltchak had received a telegram asking him to come to the assistance of the pretended Czarevitch.   I had paid no attention to these stories.

Fearing that these circumstances might give rise to difficulties, the Admiral had had the " Pretender " brought to Omsk; and General D—— had called for me, thinking that my evidence would settle the difficulty and put a stop to the legend that was beginning to grow up.

The door of the next room was opened a little, and I was able to observe, unknown to him, a boy, taller and stronger than the Czarevitch, who seemed to me fifteen or sixteen years old. His sailor's costume, the colour of his hair, and the way it was arranged were vaguely reminiscent of Alexis Nicolaïevitch. There the resemblance ended.

I told General D—— the result of my observations.   The boy was introduced to me.   I put several questions to him in French : he remained dumb.   When a reply was insisted upon he said that he understood everything I had said but had his own reasons for only speaking Russian.   I then addressed him in that language.   This, too, brought no results.   He said he had decided to answer no one but Admiral Koltchak himself.   So our interview ended.[1]

Chance had brought across my path the first of the countless pretenders who doubtless for many years to come will be a source of trouble and agitation among the ignorant and credulous masses of the Russian peasantry.

.   .   .   .   .   .

In March, 1920, I rejoined General Ditériks and N. Sokolof at Kharbine, whither they had drifted, like myself, after the collapse of Admiral Koltchak's government.   They were in a

---

[1] Shortly after my departure the bogus Czarevitch ultimately confessed the imposture.

state of great agitation, for the situation in Manchuria was growing daily more precarious, and it was expected that at any moment the Chinese eastern railway might fall into the hands of the Reds. Bolshevik spies were already beginning to swarm over the station and its surroundings. What was to be done with the documents of the enquiry? Where could they be put in safety? General Ditériks and N. Sokolof had appealed to the British High Commissioner before his departure for Pekin, asking him to take to Europe the relics of the Imperial family and the evidence of the enquiry. He had asked for instructions from his Government. The reply was a long time coming. It came at last. . . . It was in the negative!

I then appealed personally to General Janin, informing him of the situation. [1]

" I am quite ready to help you," he told me. " I can do it on my own responsibility, as there is not time to refer the matter to my Government. But it shall not be said that a French General refused the relics of one who was the faithful ally of France. Ask General Ditériks to furnish me with a written request expressing his certainty of my consent; I should consider doubt as a reflection on me."

The letter was sent, and General Ditériks came to an understanding with General Janin as to the arrangements for transmitting the precious objects to the person named by him in Europe.

Two days later, General Ditériks, his two orderly officers, N. Sokolof, and myself took on our shoulders the heavy valises prepared beforehand and carried them to General

---

[1] The French Military Mission had been gradually evacuated eastwards and was then at Kharbine.

Janin's train, which was standing a short distance from the station.   In single file we were approaching the platform when those in the rear suddenly saw several figures start up out of the shadows and accost us, shouting : " Where are you going ? What have you got in those bags ? "   As we hurried on without reply they made as if to stop us and ordered us to open our valises.   The distance that remained was fortunately not very great ; we dashed forward at full speed, and a moment later reached the General's carriage, the sentries having already run up to meet us.

At last all the evidence was in safety.   It was time, for, as had just been proved, we were marked down.   An hour later we slipped out of the train one after the other and made our way unobserved between the carriages of others standing near.

On the next day General Ditériks brought General Janin the box containing the relics of the Imperial family.

This happened on March 19th, 1920.

.   .   .   .   .   .

There was nothing now to keep me in Siberia.   I felt that I had fulfilled the last duty towards those to whom I was attached by such poignant memories. More than two years had passed since I had been separated from them at Ekaterinburg.

Ekaterinburg ! As I was leaving Russia, with what emotion I lived again, down to the least details, the painful scenes which this name called up in my mind ! Ekaterinburg to me meant the despair of feeling my every effort vain ; cruel and brutal separation ; for them it was to be the last stage of their long Calvary, two months of suffering to be endured before the supreme deliverance.

It was the period when Germany was determined to

triumph at any price and believed that victory was at last within her grasp ; and while William fraternised with Lenin, his armies were making one more thrust at Paris.

In this total collapse of Russia there were still two points of resistance ; in this abysmal night two fires remained where the flame of faith still burned bright. There was, on the one hand, General Alexeief's gallant little army of volunteers, struggling desperately against the Soviet regiments stiffened by German officers. On the other, behind the wooden enclosures which imprisoned him, the Czar, too, was leading his last fight. Supported by the Czarina, he had refused all compromise. Nothing remained but to sacrifice their lives ; they were ready to do this rather than bargain with the enemy who had ruined their country by violating its honour.

And death came, but death refused to separate those whom life had so closely bound together, and it took them all seven, united in one faith and one love.

I feel that events have spoken for themselves. Anything I might be able to add now—intensely as my feelings have been quickened by recalling those days of anguish relived sometimes from hour to hour—would appear mere vain literature and misplaced sentimentality compared with the poignant significance of the facts.

I must, however, assert here this conviction : it is impossible that those of whom I have spoken should have suffered their martyrdom in vain. I know not when it will be, nor how ; but one day or other, without any doubt, when brutality has bled itself to death in the excess of its fury, humanity will draw from the memory of their sufferings an invincible force for moral reparation.

Whatever revolt may rankle in the heart, and however

just vengeance may be, to hope for an expiation in blood would be an insult to their memory.

The Czar and Czarina died believing themselves martyrs to their country : they have died martyrs to humanity. Their real greatness is not to be measured by the prestige of their Imperial dignity, but by the wonderful moral heights to which they gradually attained. They have become a force, an ideal ; and in the very outrage they have suffered we find a touching testimony to that wonderful serenity of soul against which violence and passion can avail nothing and which triumphs unto death.

THE END